FACT AND **FALLACY**
IN AMERICAN POLITICS

Karon Penley
713 Cannon

AF689623

FACT AND **FALLACY** IN AMERICAN POLITICS

ROLAND F. MOY

Appalachian State University
Boone, North Carolina

GOODYEAR PUBLISHING COMPANY, INC.
Pacific Palisades, California

Copyright © 1973 by
GOODYEAR PUBLISHING COMPANY, INC.
Pacific Palisades, California 90272

All rights reserved. No part of this book may be reproduced in any form or by any means without permission in writing from the publisher.

Current printing (last digit):
10 9 8 7 6 5 4 3 2 1

Library of Congress Catalog Card Number:
72-97278
Y-288-4 72-97278 ISBN: 0-87620-288-1

Printed in the United States of America

Contents

Preface

For the first- or second-year college student, studying the complex process of the American political system of government can be both confusing and frustrating. Unfortunately, most high school civics courses do little more than reinforce popularly held beliefs and half-truths. Although politics is, of course, closely bound to the basic values and beliefs of a people, there are those individuals engaged directly or indirectly in political activity who often find it useful and/or expedient to deliberately exploit popular shibboleths for their own purposes—even if underlying premises are erroneous or only partly accurate.

It is argued that fostering popular notions about the American political system (such as those stated in the pledge to the flag) is useful for maintaining the stability of the political system. On the other hand, as educational opportunities are expanded and public awareness increases, disillusionment and cynicism are nurtured when the gaps between myth and reality about American politics are exposed. The discontent, the restlessness, and even the open challenges to the establishment during the past ten years can be explained, at least in part, by this kind of disillusionment. It can be argued, therefore, that fostering political realism is also an aid to political stability.

This book is designed to help correct some of the misunderstandings about American politics through the use of straightforward language and the introduction of analytic precision, however briefly stated. The comments will explore the empirical situation or make some distinctions in language or definition which are crucial to accurate evaluation and understanding.

The organization of topics reflects my conception of the kind of text supplement this book should be. From my perusal of more than a dozen American government textbooks in the past years (as a member of our textbook selection committee), a pattern of strengths and weaknesses of such texts has emerged. Most do adequately treat the preponderance of myths concerning the presidency, the Congress, political parties, and interest groups. Nevertheless, few have adequate discussions of the misconceptions involving the Declaration of Independence, the Constitution, or the application of law to achieve liberty and justice. The discussion of topics in *Fact and Fallacy in American Politics* gives special attention to these areas while covering only highlights of well-known topics in order to limit repetition.

My list of fallacies is neither exhaustive in coverage nor in depth, and is not sufficient for use as the only reading material for a course in American politics. This book is designed to help clarify critical points which, if left obscured or inaccurate, would lead to unsatisfactory analysis, irrelevant political disputation, and perhaps even the perpetuation of injustices. Achieving conceptual and logical clarity as well as empirical accuracy is basic to making worthwhile evaluations and necessary for the effective fulfillment of a citizenship or political role.

It is very difficult to determine the sources for various ideas incorporated in a text of this kind since they have been developed over several years of reading and of interaction with colleagues and students. It is possible, however, to acknowledge the assistance rendered in the immediate task of manuscript improvement. The suggestions of my present associates Marvin K. Hoffman, Richter H. Moore, Jr., and David Sutton were very helpful in formative stages. Professors David Grubbs, Richard Leach, Mario Perez-Reilly, and C. H. Richards read early drafts and offered useful suggestions, many of which were incorporated. And the editorial staff of Goodyear Publishing Company has been most helpful in suggesting improvements to make the book more useful and readable. However, the final version reflects my judgment and remains my responsibility. Neither original ideas nor suggested improvements would have reached fruition without the cooperative efforts of my wife, Jean, who typed the many drafts required along the way to completion.

FACT AND **FALLACY**
IN AMERICAN POLITICS

CHAPTER ONE

Introduction

The dictionary defines *fallacy* as an idea or opinion founded on mistaken logic or perception: it is a deceptive, misleading, or false notion or belief. Fallacious reasoning and conclusions derive from a variety of sources. Noting a few of these sources will not only provide some context for the fallacies discussed in the following chapters, but it may also furnish some guidance for making necessary distinctions in issue areas not analyzed here. These sources of error will be discussed seriatim, but in practice they often reinforce one another in shaping erroneous conclusions.

One source of error is caused by simply "taking the easy way out," either by observing or considering only readily observable features of the issue at hand, or by taking direct and immediate action without consideration of the consequences. It is often difficult to fully explore a situation to discover which background features are involved or which contributing factors are present. If a disturbance or protest occurs, for example, it is easy to conclude that better police preparation and methods would solve this type of problem. Or if a constitution of a government or organization establishes decision-making institutions, it is easy to assume that one need not look beyond these formal structures to ascertain which groups or individuals are most influential in shaping the policies that emerge in various issue areas. Prima facie examination is a good starting point for drawing conclusions or for guiding action, but deeper analysis is usually rewarding. Even if extended examination confirms initial judgments, it helps to ensure that those judgments are well-founded.

Confusing intent with practice is another source of error. For example, because separation of powers was intended to help solve the problem of injustice or majority tyranny, it does not necessarily mean that it does so in fact, in all, or even in most cases. It will usually depend upon the question involved and which criteria are used to determine which outcome is achieved. In terms of policy intent, the example of troops being sent for the purpose of "preserving freedom" in either domestic conflicts or foreign countries might be noted. Such an action, if taken, does not necessarily mean that intended results will be realized. Outcomes must be examined to discover if, in fact, policy goals have been achieved; one should not simply assume them to have been achieved because of original intent. The original goals may be achieved only in part, if at all, and secondary effects may be such that the total impact of action taken will negate the desirable results intended.

Another major source of confusion is the ethnocentric assumption that one's own country is the best and ranks first in all things worth considering. Such assumptions are encouraged by the childhood process of political socialization in which things are simplified and glorified in order to gain commitment and loyalty. Subtle, ethnocentric attitudes can lead to problems when examining the situation in the United States regarding adequate health care, the lowering of unemployment rates, economic aid to other countries, or pollution control. In all these areas there are other countries that are doing measurably better than the United States. Patriotism should not require blind acceptance of conditions or policies, especially if the country claims to be democratic.

The confusion of intent with practice and the development of ethnocentric views are both aided by the role of authoritative pronouncements in political and social life. A person who is respected because of his office or position, or because of educational or scholarly achievements, tends to receive more credence than a person without those attainments. The statements made may be accurate, but in most situations of controversy there will be more than one authoritative pronouncement on the subject and those statements will likely disagree. Governmental officials will also attempt to use their authoritative position to gain acceptance of their claims that intended policy goals have been achieved. Those in authority tend to encourage ethnocentrism by emphasizing the virtues of the system and of the policies being pursued so that system legitimacy is maintained and leadership obeyed. Many people find it inviting not to question authority, and it is probably safe to assert that the weaker the demand for substantiation of asserted claims, the greater the probability that authoritative statements will be an additional source of error.

Confusing form and substance leads to many pitfalls. While it is true that form or patterns of doing things can affect policy outputs and sociopolitical outcomes, it is important to ascertain under which conditions form makes a significant impact on substance. Such distinctions must be made when considering the form and structure of American national government, including separation of powers and federalism. These features are often assumed to be necessary to preserve the substance of democracy and the free society. But this ignores the essential or defining features of democracy and the fact that other forms of national government organization are compatible with democratic decision making and freedoms. Again, a certain amount of unconscious ethnocentrism tends to creep in. The structures of government used in the United States are assumed to be the best and so interrelated that modifications in any part of the formal structure—such as in our present federal system—would necessarily do away with democracy. Such is not the case, as will be explained at greater length elsewhere in this volume.

A continuing problem for policy or system evaluation is obsolescence of conceptual frameworks. All of us have psychological mind sets which help us to structure and understand the reality which we perceive. These mind sets incorporate both empirically verifiable facts and our personal evaluation of them. From these combinations come the generalizations about social and political life that we accept as true and which guide our judgment of events and policies. In international affairs, for example, we form generalizations about whether or not the communist systems of the world are a monolithic and united bloc, or whether the appeasement of Hitler at Munich in 1939 is relevant to today's problems of guerrilla warfare. On the domestic scene people form general ideas, based upon past relationships, about the proper role of government in relation to the economy and society. In all these cases, the generalizations and conclusions are formed on the basis of the empirical evidence available at some point in time. But these generalizations and conclusions have a tendency to persist even though conditions change. They persist because the persons formulating or advocating these views have a continued role in opinion leadership and policy making over a long period of time. They persist because of the continued reference to past events as analogous and therefore relevant for contemporary events. They persist because the socialization and education processes encourage the acceptance of the dominant frameworks of thought. Although personal values may remain constant, empirical conditions do change. As conditions change, historical analogies become more difficult to apply without modification. Such historical changes, therefore, make it probable that old generalizations or conceptual frameworks, which once aided in the understanding of reality, may be outmoded and in need of reformulation to prevent a distorted view of the world. When such adjustments are not made, the groundwork is laid for fallacious reasoning regarding current events.

A major source of difficulty in accurate analysis is a failure to distinguish empirical, normative, and legal statements. *Empirical statements are statements of fact.* They are descriptive of what is now factually the case or what was, in fact, the situation previously. Statements referring to future situations that may be tested for their factual basis are also empirical. Conclusions are reached through a more or less rigorous application of scientific methods of examining the evidence. Although the problem of personal selectivity of factual data is always present, a premise of scientific analysis holds that given the same set of data or evidence and definitions of terms, reasonable men would tend to agree on the facts of a case. They may disagree on the meaning of the facts or their implications for policy, but that is a different question which involves personal judgment and preferences.

Normative statements are expressed value preferences or beliefs about what ought to be true or should be the goal, even if in fact the situation that exists is not the one preferred. Such value preferences are not subject to the usual verification procedures of scientific investigation as in the case of empirical statements. They are usually based upon religious doctrine, philosophic and theological inquiry, or intuition. Value preferences, such as belief in individual dignity or human equality, are important for every person and give meaning and purpose to life and living. In social and political affairs, values shape the goals that are pursued and the type of government that is possible. Determining which values are better, preferable, or more adequate, however, is a difficult task that usually requires a combination of empirical data on what is possible—the assumption is that if something *ought* to be, it *can* be—and data on the comparative consequences of different values. Moreover this information must be combined with some insight into the needs, traditions, or nature of human beings in their cultural and universal environment. It is useful in normative considerations to give greater weight to informed, scholarly value judgments than to uninformed, unreflective opinions. But people will still differ on which values are preferable. They will also differ on priorities among a number of values and on interpretations for application of the same value. Because mass opinions have political consequences, such differences will have an important impact upon peaceful resolution of political disputes which usually include considerations of both facts and values.

Legal statements or provisions are rules of conduct which are backed by the authority and power of the government. However a distinction should be made between what is legal, what is moral or normatively preferred, and what is empirically verified. It is not necessarily true that legally enforceable rules are also normatively desirable and followed in practice. If there were no discrepancies between laws, values, and practice it would be a perfect or utopian society, a situation not yet achieved in history. That which is defined as legal, in terms of constitutional interpretation and statutory law, may accurately describe empirical reality insofar as the law is obeyed. Since compliance with laws is seldom universal, however, there will always be some discrepancy between legal provisions and actual practice. To gain an understanding of how a political system functions or how laws are applied, therefore, it is not enough to read constitutional provisions or statutory law. This information will not be sufficient to determine actual practice, which may deviate from the spirit and/or letter of the law. For example, the Constitution of the United States guarantees "equal protection of the laws" and there are statutes such as those forbidding racial discrimination in the use of public facilities, which attempt to provide this protection. Despite the constitutional clause and the statutory enforcement provisions, there still exists a degree of racial discrimination which a reading of the Constitution and of related laws would not reveal. Fallacious reasoning results when one accepts laws as being descriptive of reality when he should determine the extent of the gap between legal descriptions and reality.

It should be noted that interpretation of the meaning of broad provisions like "equal protection of the laws" will vary from decade to decade and from person to person as well. In part this results from the fact that each individual has a set of value preferences or goals which he thinks important. Most people prefer that the laws under which they live embody or advance their values. Therefore, if the laws are compatible there is no problem. If, however, a law, or policy having the effect of law, is in conflict with personal values, the potential for political dispute is increased. Some people will take action to change the law or policy and will attempt to bring what is legally enforced into line with normative convictions. There is, however, no guarantee of success. The point is that laws establish rules of conduct which, if violated, legally subject the violator to the sanctions of governmental control. Such laws may be regarded as moral by most citizens, but not everyone will agree.

One factor usually involved in forming erroneous conclusions is the failure to employ logical reasoning. A full exposition of logical reasoning and relationships cannot be attempted here, but a few types of error in deductive reasoning can be noted. It is often assumed that the truth of a conclusion is established if the conclusion is logically derived from the premises. But logical validity is only one factor in establishing the truth of conclusions. We can be sure that the conclusion is true only if empirical analysis establishes that the premises are true, and the conclusion follows logically from those premises. Consider the following example. All democracies have federal systems and the United States is a democracy; therefore, the United States has a federal system. This is a logical (valid) argument and the conclusion is true—but the first premise is false. All democracies do not have federal systems. Now let us examine the reverse. The United States has a federal system and is also a democracy; therefore, all federal systems are democracies. Here the premises are true but it is an invalid (illogical) argument and the conclusion is false. Or, consider this argument. All members of the Senate have great responsibilities and J. William Fulbright has great responsibilities; therefore, J. William Fulbright is a senator. The premises and the conclusion are true, but it is not a logical argument. The conclusion is not implied by the premises. These examples of *deductive* logic should be enough to illustrate some of the pitfalls involved. The problems of *inductive* logic, on the other hand, are those of scientific investigation. Some of the problems involved in this type of reasoning were noted above in the discussion of empirical analysis.

The final source of error in political analysis discussed here is that which results from the everyday practice of politics. Politicians, journalists, public speakers, authors, and most people from time to time make attempts to influence the outcome of events and the making of governmental policy. The usual approach is to present arguments that favor one's position rather than to present a balanced assessment of a situation. In the process of doing this it is often convenient to leave the premises of one's argument vague or unstated, to overlook certain facts, and to fail in making careful distinctions between facts and values or between legal interpretation and values. Oftentimes it is convenient to ignore unpleasant implications or consequences of the policies advocated. While we cannot expect to consider every conceivable aspect of a problem, the usual political speech or argument is much less balanced than a scholarly analysis and geared more for emotional impact than rational persuasion. Over a period of time several consequences of this type of political argumentation emerge. First, issues become clouded or confused (Did we win in Vietnam?); moreover, definitions of terms become inconsistent (Are we really democratic?); finally, value statements become confused with other statements (The government has no right to impose wage and price controls.). At times misleading statements are made deliberately for political advantage, creating the credibility gap which is charged to some political leaders. Careful analysis of issues and policies should help detect the errors and misleading information that are presented for mass consumption. This book is intended as an aid in that kind of careful analysis.

A NOTE ON FALLACY SELECTION

The fallacies included in this volume were chosen to enhance its function as a textbook supplement. Chapters Two, Three, and Four are more extensive than other chapters because most textbooks are rather brief in covering these topics, while Chapters Five, Six, and Seven are limited in scope because most textbooks provide adequate presentations of these subjects. Some of the fallacies may appear to be overstated in a negative sense, yet *this is the way in which they are often communicated.* It appears reasonable, then, to state the fallacies in the terms in which they are encountered.

Some of the fallacies may appear to be merely minor variations of others which are also discussed. These items are included to emphasize topics (or cliches) which are encountered in just those terms in the world of politics. In this way, it is hoped, the error of each fallacy, in all its forms, is more easily identified and the point remembered. The discussion of each fallacy is also meant, as far as possible, to be self-contained, especially when read in the light of the comments in this introduction. This should enable the reader to open the volume to any topic and understand the point of the analysis, with little, if any, reference to other fallacies.

The selected references at the end of each chapter have two purposes. The first is to identify a limited range of research which provides the empirical and analytic base for most of the topics covered in each chapter, while briefly noting the major relevant points of each book. The second purpose is to encourage further reading on these topics in sources that, for the most part are both readily available and easily comprehensible for the beginning student.

CHAPTER TWO

Political Analysis: Values, Stability, Democracy

FALLACY 1

"All men are created equal" is a factually correct statement.

Empirical (factual) evidence indicates that men are unequal in many observable or measurable ways, including those of mental ability, physical capacity or talent, and occupational accomplishments. Even at birth human beings exhibit inequalities in physical and mental capability. The assertion as stated in the Declaration of Independence that "all men are created equal" is, therefore, not based upon empirical evidence, but is a value statement. It expresses the belief in the essential equality of persons as human beings despite their many observable inequalities and differences. It is a NORMATIVE or VALUE statement of principle which argues that men ought to be considered inherently equal (equally human) and therefore equally deserving of that respect for human dignity which might be expected from persons of equal standing.

Unlike an empirical statement, it is very difficult to determine if a normative statement is correct, since there is little evidence for or against it that can be produced to convince reasonable men of its soundness. People do accept such value statements, however, and the general acceptance of such principles is the basis of social and political organization and practice. The belief in human equality, for example, is one basis for justifying equal voting rights in democratic political systems and equal protection of the law.

FALLACY 2

People who accept the same values and principles are seldom in political disagreement, so it is relatively easy to tell our friends from our enemies.

People accept many principles such as a belief in human equality and individual liberty. They also place great value on such things as social order and national security. Even if everyone in a society accepted these values and principles they would still tend to have political disagreements, since political decisions involve the selection of a *priority* in values and an *interpretation* of how a value or principle applies in a particular case.

Among people who accept the same values there will tend to be differences among them in ranking the values according to importance. Such differences in priority will mean that on a given issue some persons will consider social order more important than individual rights or liberty. Such an issue sometimes arises when people protest a governmental policy. Is it more important to protect the liberty of those who protest —even though the protest might disturb other people—or is it more important to preserve public calm and order? In the case of a person accused of a crime, is it more important to have strict standards of evidence which give greater protection to the individual's right to a fair trial —even though some guilty persons might go free—or is it more important to relax standards of evidence to gain more convictions so that society as a whole might better be protected—even though some innocent persons are found guilty? There is no easy answer to these questions of priority and reasonable men can and do disagree.

Another issue area may generate disagreement about whether equality or national security is more important. Some people believe that a large portion of the national budget should be spent on military hardware and research in a top priority attempt to preserve an American military capability which would enable the United States to maintain a nuclear force superior to that of the Soviet Union, and which would also preserve the ability to provide massive support for military struggles in distant countries to preserve friendly governments in power. Others think that a few less billions should be spent for military defense and warfare and more spent in this country to improve living conditions by equalizing opportunities for education, health care, and employment. Again, people will disagree on policy options even though they all agree that both national defense capability and adequate living standards are needed or desirable.

Even if there is agreement on priorities there may still be disagreement over which policy option best satisfies the priority. This kind of disagreement arises because of differences in interpretation of what a value such as equality or individual liberty means in a particular case, and because there is usually insufficient empirical or factual information concerning the relevance or effects of various policy alternatives. In the school busing controversy, for example, does equal educational opportunity *require* busing of some children across old school district lines, and does this requirement constitute an infringement of individual liberty? Congress has passed legislation calling for a moratorium on busing in apparent agreement with the second half of the question. But political conflict has developed over these and other interpretive issues as various persons and groups advance their point of view in an attempt to influence political decisions, despite a stated acceptance of the same values or even the same priority. Just because someone disagrees with us on policy, therefore, does not necessarily mean that he does not share our basic system values or is not a loyal American. To determine whether there is fundamental disagreement on values requires more than evidence of mere disagreement on policy.

FALLACY 3

The only way to solve the problem of protest and occasional disruption of the political system is to improve law enforcement efficiency and effectiveness.

Political protest arises for a variety of reasons, but a primary one is that a conflict over policies often leads one side of the struggle to make public appeals and to demonstrate in an attempt to publicize and rally support for a particular point of view. These public protest efforts become disruptive at times and restrict or infringe on the liberties or rights of other people when they block free movement or damage property. For some, dissatisfaction with the system may become sufficiently strong to cause them to abandon the use of protest methods to gain adoption of their policy within the political system. These persons decide that, even in the long run, their reform efforts will be futile, and they may attempt to work against the system itself in hopes of bringing about its collapse or radical alteration.

People support a system of government basically for one, or a combination of three reasons. Apart from those who are apathetic and support the system by default, (1) the policy output of the system over a period of time satisfies them sufficiently if not entirely, (2) the system is held to have high legitimacy for its own sake even if few demands are satisfied, or (3) they are compelled to support the system by threats—power—or by actual application of sanctions or punishment—force. Except for those few who already reject the system, it does not follow that the only way to solve the problem of protest and occasional disruption is by more efficient law enforcement. A change in policy which would satisfy at least some of the demands being made could also solve the problem. Governmental leaders could establish procedures for broader participation in political decisions, especially for those who feel alienated from the system, or they could at least demonstrate concern for the problems causing the complaint and promise to try to alleviate the situation. These actions, including symbolic gestures of concern, would tend to increase support for the political system in a way that avoids compulsion and help to forestall system rejection by the dissatisfied. These responses to protest would not only help maintain system stability but, by using persuasion rather than threats or force, would also produce policies more congenial to democratic spirit and practice.

FALLACY 4

Understanding the legal requirements of a written constitution and the laws of a nation will reveal how the political system works.

This would be true only if there were clearly defined legal provisions guiding all politically relevant behavior, and these provisions were always followed. In the practical world of politics men are guided not only by law but also by tradition and by the requirements of particular situations on which the law may be silent or ambiguous. In the United States, for example, political parties developed and influenced political activity long before legal restraints were placed upon some of their activities, and the unit rule in presidential electoral voting, which gives all of the electoral votes of a state to the winner of the popular vote, is still a traditional rule in most states.

Even if there are written legal requirements to guide officials the rules may be ignored or evaded. In some countries a written constitution is viewed only as an ideal which need not be followed in practice; if the ruling elite is in a position to do so the rules may be made up as the need requires with no provision for meeting constitutional requirements of due process or substantive rights. Laws are evaded or violated all the time to some degree in all countries. In the United States, for example, few major political campaigns are conducted which strictly adhere to the restrictions on campaign contributions or expenditures.

Because factors such as tradition, expediency, and illegal evasion affect the operation of political systems, there will be a discrepancy between the legal outlines of politics and government and the empirical practice thereof. In addition, there will usually be a discrepancy between normative ideals of what ought to be done and that which is actually done. Therefore, an examination of a political system which relies exclusively upon legal analysis and ignores political behavior will be incomplete and misleading.

FALLACY 5

Democratic government requires a written constitution which spells out the limits, ends, and structure of government.

Most modern democracies have written constitutions. This is because nearly all of them, at some point in history, have been deliberately established as systems employing democratic political principles. It was felt necessary to produce a written document which would specify those principles and structural features which would satisfy the varied interest of the founders and serve as a unifying instrument to stabilize the newly established system.

Not all democracies, however, have followed this path. The most obvious case in point is Great Britain. Their democracy is not guided by the outlines of any one major document produced at one point in time, subject to later modification and interpretation. Rather, their constitution is a combination of specialized documents (e.g., the Magna Charta and the 1689 Bill of Rights), legislation passed by the government (such as that which spells out the powers of the House of Lords), traditional practices (e.g., the requirement that the prime minister be a member of the House of Commons), and court decisions. There are no legal constitutional restrictions on what the government may enact into law such as a court which reviews legislation to determine constitutionality. However, this does not mean that the British government may enact into law anything it chooses, because contemporary standards, appropriate expectations, and/or tradition impose limits upon governmental arbitrariness or innovation. In practice, such expectations and commitments to accepted standards, especially among social and political elites, are the effective barriers to government abuses of authority in all democratic systems, regardless of whether or not a written constitution exists. A written statement of principles is only as good as the strength of commitment to those principles. The Soviet Union and many Latin American republics have written constitutions containing statements of principle which could be used to make democracy effective; but there is little commitment to these principles, and thus the written constitution is a dead letter.

It may be useful then, to distinguish between the *written* constitution and what might be called the *effective* constitution, and to note three patterns of relationship between them and democracy. Those principles and methods of operation actually supported and in use form the limits, ends, and structure of the effective constitution. If the effective constitution is not a distortion or evasion of a written democratic constitution, so much the better for people committed to democratic principles. If, second, the effective constitution, which tends to be sustained primarily by the commitments and expectations of the people controlling the political systems, does not respect democratic principles, it will be of little use in the struggle to restrain government (except, perhaps, over an extended period of time) to spell out those principles in a written document. Finally, if the effective constitution is already democratic in character, little is gained in the struggle to preserve democratic rights and liberties by having a written constitution, unless there is a need to bring various democratic factions together in some common agreement on principles as in the establishment of a new state.

FALLACY 6

Lincoln was accurate in defining the essential democratic characteristics of the American system when he stated that it is a system of government "of the people, by the people, and for the people."

This famous statement has a figurative element of truth which gives it power to rally support for a threatened political system, which it was intended to do. But taken literally, as too often happens, Lincoln's statement is misleading and irrelevant. While it is true that democracy permits broad popular participation in politics and government, and generally produces policies that benefit most people, it is in the details of how people participate in making beneficial policies that determines democratic character. Ignoring these details makes the statement misleading to many people around the world and irrelevant to understanding what is or is not essential for democracy.

While nearly all governments in the world claim to be "of the people" by legitimizing themselves through asserting that they rule in the name of the people, no major government is in fact run "by the people." Most governments claim to be governing "for the people," or for their benefit. What differentiates democracy from other forms of government, however, is the specific way in which people participate. Democracy in large systems involves not the direct participation of the people in day-to-day decision making, but involves the broad popular participation of the people in a freely competitive process of choosing elected representatives and influencing political decisions by organizing to promote and publicize policy alternatives. Most of the governments of the world claim to be democratic, but few permit the system to operate with this democratic style. It is this style which distinguishes democracy as a specific type of government, not whether it is simply of the people, by the people, and for the people.

FALLACY 7

Government operated for the general interest of the people is also democratic.

Leaders who govern in the best interest of the people could be wise kings, benevolent dictators, or lucky democratic representatives. Wise and rational policies are desirable, but democracy may or may not provide them, although it is assumed in terms of democratic principles that the people generally know what is best for them. The democratic method ensures that elected leaders will be responsive to broad popular interests, but leaders may be at least somewhat responsive without achieving office through democratic means (e.g., the Shah of Iran and President Tito of Yugoslavia).

FALLACY 8

Periodic elections in a democracy establish the truth of a particular policy or position.

Truth may or may not be popular. While democratic elections help to prevent abuses associated with the imposition of some particular view of "truth" by an elite (such as the abuses demonstrated in heresy trials in early American colonial times), and such elections may result at times in what is demonstrated to be a rational policy, there is no one-to-one correlation between election popularity and rationality or truth. Men can be, and have been, elected to office even though they advocate policies that are irrational or based upon a fallacy. Majorities can be misled, and only a constant effort to explore and test policy alternatives can help to produce more rational political action.

FALLACY 9

Democracy means that the majority rules in all cases.

In the absence of divine guidance or infallible rationality, the majority principle for making political decisions is a convenient expedient for determining whose will is to prevail. This does not mean that all decisions are made by majorities, or that democracies permit majorities to do anything they wish.

A majority, or 50 percent plus one, is the usual requirement in legislative voting, but many decisions are made by other standards. Election to office usually requires only a plurality, meaning more votes than any one other candidate—not a majority. It is interesting to note, for example, that 15 presidents have been elected who did not receive a majority of the popular vote cast, including President Nixon in 1968, and that three of them received fewer popular votes than their major opponent and won office by a majority vote in the House of Representatives (Thomas Jefferson and John Quincy Adams) or by a disputed majority of the electoral college vote (Rutherford B. Hayes). Some decisions, such as passing a constitutional amendment or stopping debate in the Senate, require an extraordinary majority of two-thirds or three-fourths to pass. Many decisions in government are made by minorities, whether of one or a few: presidential decisions, many executive agency decisions, and decisions by congressional committee chairmen—important decisions which can either block or expedite government action. It should also be made clear that decisions made by governmental officials may or may not have the support of the majority of the voting population, since popularity is only one of several factors considered by political leaders when making decisions.

Studies of historical trends have shown that in democracies persistent majorities tend to have their way. But although the majority principle used to arrive at *some* decisions makes this possible, there must be limits on what majorities may decide if the system is to remain democratic. The basic limits are those which protect the liberty of various minority interests or groups to engage in active, public, and peaceful political opposition to the majority position on any issue. In this way they can attempt to become part of a new majority on one or more issues. To the degree that these liberties are curtailed directly or indirectly through the forces of majority opinion by legal or social means, the requisite, defining, and therefore essential characteristics of democracy will be impaired or destroyed. In other words, if these limits on majority action are not respected, a majority could apply pressures or vote for measures that would bring an end to democracy for that system.

FALLACY 10

Democracy means equality in all things.

Democracy requires equality in *some* things. Specifically, it requires equal political rights, such as the right to vote and the right to run for elective office in a freely competitive situation; and it requires equal legal rights, such as equal justice under law or equal protection of the law. All democracies have had difficulty in upholding these rights for all citizens, but all systems of government are less than ideal in practice. Ideals themselves change, of course, and the definition of what legal or political rights ought to be may change as they relate to special distinctions. These distinctions may be based upon such things as race, sex, or religion which can affect many aspects of life such as voting rights, judicial proceedings, and political or religious expression and practice. In the United States, for example, the rights of blacks and of women have expanded in the past century, and are continuing to expand as the legal definitions of equality are modified and expanded.

In his critique of those who consider democracy as merely a method for holding political leaders accountable, Peter Bachrach includes equality of political power as an additional essential feature of democracy. He believes that participation in decisions not only safeguards interests in terms of policies made, but that participation also enhances human dignity and is, therefore, a goal worth achieving. While agreeing that equality of political power and participation is a worthwhile goal, it would appear that such a goal cannot be achieved, or even approached, unless the democratic method of choosing leaders is preserved. The method is a prior requisite or necessary condition for achieving the goal. There can be a democratic choice of leaders without equality of political power in a large political system, in the sense that competing elites can be held accountable to the masses of people by periodic electoral competition. But there would appear to be a small probability of success in attempting to improve equality of political power without the basic rights and procedures of the democratic method. The essential requirements for democracy, then, are contained in the rights and procedures associated with the democratic method of holding leaders accountable. They do not necessarily include other goals, such as the equalization of political influence, made possible by the successful functioning of a democratic system.

Democracy does *not* require equality in social standing or economic possessions. However, it has increasingly been believed in most democratic systems that the government has an obligation to ensure that everyone has an equal opportunity to develop whatever talents or skills that person possesses. This can be accomplished by a variety of measures including the equalization of educational opportunities, the regulation of employment discrimination and unfair business competition, and the establishment of aid programs to ensure that no person becomes mentally or physically handicapped because of avoidable inadequacies in food, health care, or social environment. These governmental efforts would not cause all persons to become equal in all things. Quite to the contrary, the best would still emerge at the top of various ladders of achievement. But such programs would ensure that those at the top were there not because of advantages of wealth, outside influence, or inheritance, but because they deserved to be there through demonstrated ability in a situation of equal opportunity.

In conclusion it should be noted that, as a practical matter, the stability of democratic systems is improved if sharp and unbridgeable gaps between the rich and the poor do not exist. Empirical studies of democratic systems support the conclusion that democracy works best where a large middle class exists and people have the opportunity to achieve a middle-class standard of living. So although democracy requires only political and legal equality in terms of rights, such rights are more likely to survive in practice if there is some degree of social and economic equality.

FALLACY 11

If political leaders are elected or approved by popular vote, the system is democratic.

Modern democracy uses the representative principle to facilitate the governing of large numbers of people. Although the representative principle is a necessary condition for modern democracy, it is not by itself a sufficient condition. Many systems of government, including those of the Soviet Union and the People's Republic of China, have representatives who are elected by popular vote, but we do not consider them democratic. There are also numerous examples of political leaders or dictators who submit issues (such as the question of their continued rule) to a vote of the people in a plebiscite which is conducted in controlled conditions to minimize opposition and assure a favorable vote of confidence.

In addition to the need for elected representatives, modern democracy requires that persons standing for office compete with one another in free and open opposition so that the voters will have a choice between broadly defined policy positions. This implies the freedom to organize an opposition and the freedom to speak out on the issues in an attempt to rally public support. It also implies that the political rights of those in a minority position will be respected so that they may continue to offer organized, public, and peaceful opposition to those who may currently hold majority favor.

FALLACY 12

The existence of several political parties in a country indicates that it has a democratic system.

The existence of two or more political parties in a political system is one indicator of a democratic system, but this alone is not sufficient evidence.

It would be necessary to know the extent of competition for office between those parties, and how freely they are allowed to operate in rallying support for their policies. It would also be useful to know how much competition is allowed within each party in the selection of party leaders. The People's Republic of China, for example, has more than one political party, but the political system is almost completely dominated by the Communist Party. Bolivia, Argentina, and Brazil have a number of political parties, but their presence is largely irrelevant in terms of choosing political leadership or offering opposition to official policy. The freedom to compete for office and for policy acceptance is essential for democracy. To the extent that restrictions are placed upon opposition or peaceful party competition, the existence of two or more parties is an inaccurate indicator of democracy.

FALLACY 13

If a government or ruling group enjoys wide popularity it is also democratic.

Not necessarily. Many nondemocratic national political leaders actually attract broad popular support or claim to receive it. Throughout history there have been popular monarchs, such as Solomon and Elizabeth I, or dictators, such as Napoleon III and Ho Chi Minh, who could probably have won a popular election or vote of confidence during their tenure in office. On the other hand there have been democratically elected leaders who, while in office, lost their popularity with a majority of the citizenry. Recently, President Lyndon Johnson of the United States and President Charles DeGaulle of France declined from favor while in office.

While it is true that democracy implies that elected leaders enjoy fairly wide popularity, the reverse relationship of popularity implying democracy does not necessarily hold. Many political leaders around the world attempt to equate popularity with democracy, but unless these leaders are elected by democratic means, their claim is a mere effort to cloak their position of power with attractive labels.

FALLACY 14

If government is to remain democratic it must protect unalienable rights of life, liberty, and property.

No government in practice protects unalienable (natural or absolute) rights to anything, and even in theory such a government would be possible only among angels, in which case government would be unnecessary. To govern means to limit or restrain people from doing that which they would otherwise do in the absence of government; that which would interfere with the considered good order of the total society. Even democracies put life in jeopardy by requiring military service; limit property rights by taxation and eminent domain; and circumscribe liberty by restrictions of many kinds, such as restraints on religious practice and/or on the freedom to belong to groups of one's choice without threat of official penalty or harassment.

Democracy requires, as a basic minimum, that restraints on rights be of such character that they do not unduly interfere with the formation of peaceful political opposition to those in power. The rights which enable a minority political party to make public appeals in an attempt to become a majority party or part of a majority coalition must be maintained, and could be considered fundamental rights of democracy. This does not mean, however, that some restrictions for the sake of public order may not be placed upon appeals which may lead to violent behavior. Such restrictions would be impossible, however, if the government operated on the principle that rights were unalienable.

People can and do criticize governmental regulations that they consider to be an infringement of unalienable rights. Such criticism is useful in a democracy and is part of the never-ending debate on where the line should be drawn between liberty and restraint. But if government is to govern, of necessity it must have the authority to draw a line by reserving the right to set limits even if some people dislike the decision. In a democracy such limits would in general reflect the dominant opinion generated by each issue. But these limits would also be subject to public scrutiny and debate in order to permit appeals by those who believe that they are unjust and want to change them.

FALLACY 15

It is impossible for a country to be both democratic and socialistic.

Democracy is a style of government and socialism is a style of economic operation, and there are many patterns possible in the relationship of government and the economy. Democracy implies that those who make the political decisions affecting our lives should be held responsible through competitive elections to those people whose lives are affected. Socialism has many meanings, but the view generally held by governing socialist parties in Western European democracies is that those making decisions in business enterprises should be guided or controlled so that their decisions fit into the overall economic policy goals of the nation as established by the government. This guidance or control does not require governmental ownership of economic enterprises, but can be effected by tax policy and governmental regulation of such things as wages and prices. These decisions are made in consultation with management and labor leaders, but the ultimate responsibility for decisions rests with the government, which in turn is responsible to the people. The British, French, Swedish and West German systems all use some variation of this political-economic relationship, as does the United States to a lesser extent with such policies as minimum wage standards and wage and price increase guidelines.

This type of relationship between the political system and the economic system is, as mentioned above, only one among many. A capitalist economic system, for example, which in principle does not hold economic decision makers responsible to the economic policy plans of government is also compatible with a democratic political system. But capitalism is also compatible with a dictatorial or nondemocratic system of government, as is socialism. There is, therefore, no necessary incompatibility between socialism and democracy nor any necessary relationship between democracy and any particular economic system.

SELECTED REFERENCES FOR FURTHER STUDY

Almond, Gabriel, and Powell, G. Bingham. *Comparative Politics: A Developmental Approach.* Boston: Little, Brown and Co., 1966.

Using a systems analysis approach, Almond and Powell demonstrate how political systems may be compared as they change over a period of time. In particular, they focus upon differentiation of structures, secularization of culture, and the possibility of subsystem autonomy. They also indicate the usefulness of evaluating system stability in terms of capabilities to perform functions of regulation, extraction of resources, and distribution of resources. General responsiveness in both practical and symbolic terms is also examined. Understanding these relationships as they apply to all political systems, including democracies, enables one to better understand specific problems such as what is involved in maintaining law and order.

Bachrach, Peter. *The Theory of Democratic Elitism: A Critique.* Boston: Little, Brown and Co., 1967.

This is an attack upon those theorists of democracy who accept as necessary, if not desirable, the fact that democracies in the United States and elsewhere are largely controlled by elites and not by a broad spectrum of the population. Bachrach rejects the notion of democracy as a mere method by which elites are held accountable by periodic free elections. He wishes democracy to be understood as a system providing rather easy, if not direct, participation by the people in all decisions which have broad social consequences at all levels of society. He states that such participation would be valuable, not just because it would keep decision making responsive, but because such participation would facilitate the growth of self-esteem and a fuller affirmation of personality for those who do take part in community decisions.

Braybrooke, David. *Three Tests for Democracy: Personal Rights, Human Welfare, Collective Preference.* New York: Random House, 1968.

Braybrooke offers interesting and philosophic discussions of three tests or standards which, among others, have been used by people to evaluate governments. He offers an argument defending the concept of inalienable rights, and discusses the writings of John Locke in this regard. In offering qualifications to Locke, and in discussing how in practice governments deal with rights, the gap between his position and that discussed in fallacy number 14 is not very great. In his discussion of collective preference and majority rule he deals primarily with the impact of party politics upon policy output, and notes that even if policy is generally in accordance with majority preference it still may violate personal rights or human welfare.

Dahl, Robert A. *A Preface to Democratic Theory.* Chicago: University of Chicago Press, 1956.

This is an extended analysis of the specific topic of an appropriate definition of democracy. Dahl prefers the term polyarchy to denote a system type that is based upon the characteristics common to political systems that are usually called democratic. The theory of polyarchy that is developed embodies a series of logically related propositions which include such things as majority decision making, political equality, and freedom of opposition. The model of democracy developed is an ideal type approximated by many political systems but perfectly attained by none.

Dahl, Robert A. *Modern Political Analysis.* Englewood Cliffs, N.J.: Prentice-Hall, 1963.

Dahl offers a wide range of definitions, analytic distinctions, and empirical observations which facilitate the understanding of complex political systems. Among the topics covered are the differentiation of political systems and economic systems, the role of legitimacy in system stability, the distinctive features of democracy, and the role of values in political analysis.

Easton, David. *A Systems Analysis of Political Life.* New York: John Wiley & Sons, 1965.

The analysis framework developed in this work is a detailed examination of the range of factors which affect political policy outputs, system support, and system stability. It attempts to identify in generally applicable terms all those factors which are relevant to politics, regardless of whether they are incorporated into constitutional law, statutory law, or the range of events that one might traditionally associate with politics.

Ebenstein, William. *Today's Isms: Communism, Fascism, Capitalism, Socialism.* 6th ed. Englewood Cliffs, N.J.: Prentice-Hall, 1970.

As the title indicates, this is an analysis and comparison of the theoretical justifications and patterns of operation of major systems of political and economic practice experienced primarily in the Western world in the twentieth century. A general conclusion is that democratic political practice is compatible with capitalism and socialism, but not with communism or fascism.

Lipset, Seymour Martin. *Political Man.* Garden City, N.Y.: Doubleday and Co., 1960.

Drawing upon data from many political systems, Lipset develops some interesting propositions concerning requisites for democracy, consensus and cleavage patterns, and problems of political stability. One of the important requisites for democracy, he finds, is a well-developed economic base which provides sufficient technology, education, and communications to allow for personal satisfaction, social mobility, and mass popular participation in the political process.

MacIver, Robert M. *The Web of Government.* New York: Macmillan Co., 1947.

MacIver discusses a wide range of historical situations to illustrate various patterns of government in relation to society. He notes the importance of a mass-based sense of community as a requisite for government and stresses that government should be considered as an instrument for dealing with those social problems which confront the community. The democratic mechanism is presented as the best means for arriving at a collective judgment about the course government should take.

Mayo, Henry B. *An Introduction to Democratic Theory.* New York: Oxford University Press, 1960.

Mayo presents an analysis to sort out various definitions of democracy and to refine our understanding of it. He confines the definition to the features of the political system, as opposed to other areas of social life, and agrees with the idea of democracy as a method or process of choosing leaders and of making decisions through competitive public involvement. He also notes the historical context of this view of democracy and notes some of the limitations of public or majority participation in democratic choice in attempting to achieve desirable policy decisions.

Moy, Roland F. *A Computer Simulation of Democratic Political Development: Tests of the Lipset and Moore Models.* Beverly Hills, Calif.: Sage Publications, 1971.

This is a study which applies a series of tests to two theories which attempt to explain the conditions under which democracy will become or remain a viable system of government. A number of propositions is developed relating democratic stability to economic growth rates, value patterns, and relative power positions.

Sargent, Lyman Tower. *Contemporary Political Ideologies: A Comparative Analysis.* Homewood, Ill.: Dorsey Press, 1969.

This is a comparative analysis of nationalism, communism, democracy, fascism, national socialism, anarchism, and the ideologies of developing nations. Common questions are posed for each ideology to facilitate an understanding of how each would deal with similar social problems and subsystem patterns. His analysis of the essential features of democracy and of political and economic relationships is most pertinent for this chapter.

Schattschneider, E. E. *The Semisovereign People: A Realist's View of Democracy in America.* New York: Holt, Rinehart and Winston, 1960.

The aspect of this book that is most relevant for our purposes is Schattschneider's discussion of the importance of competition in a democracy as a means which permits a wide range of people to participate, at least indirectly, in governmental decision making. He calls this process the socialization of conflict, and notes that each issue in the political process will have a different scope of social conflict, depending upon the interest and strategy of those who will be affected by the impending governmental action.

Spitz, David. *Patterns of Anti-Democratic Thought.* New York: The Free Press, 1965.

Democracy is defined as a system of government which holds the rulers responsible to the ruled through competitive elections and the free play of conflicting ideas. Contrary views that democracy is either impossible or undesirable are examined and found to be unpersuasive or to offer no better solution to the problems of government. Key concepts important for democracy are examined in the course of the analysis, including equality, individual liberty, majority rule, and the relative wisdom of policy output produced by the democratic process.

The following journal articles are part of the ongoing analysis of some of the topics examined in this chapter.

Buchanan, James M. "Equality as Fact and Norm." *Ethics* 81 (April 1971): 228–40.

Eisinger, Peter K. "Protest Behavior and the Integration of Urban Political Systems." *Journal of Politics* 33 (Nov. 1971):980–1007.

Elcock, H. J. "Justice and the Political Order." *Political Studies* 17 (Sept. 1969): 294–312.

Mann, Michael. "Social Cohesion of Liberal Democracy." *American Sociological Review* 35 (June 1970):423–39.

May, John D. "Inequality Abets Democracy?" *Ethics* 80 (July 1970):266–78.
Medding, Peter Y. " 'Elitist' Democracy: An Unsuccessful Critique of a Misunderstood Theory." *Journal of Politics* 31 (Aug. 1969):641–54.
Ricci, David M. "Democracy Attenuated: Schumpeter, the Process Theory, and American Democratic Thought." *Journal of Politics* 32 (May 1970):239–67.
Weinstein, Michael A. "Critique of Contemporary Democratic Theories." *Western Political Quarterly* 24 (March 1971):41–44.
Wilson, John. "Towards a Society of Friends: Some Reflections on the Meaning of Democratic Socialism." *Canadian Journal of Political Science* 3 (Dec. 1970): 628–54.

CHAPTER THREE

The Declaration of Independence and the United States Constitution

FALLACY 16

The principles stated by the Declaration of Independence establish rights which the United States government is obligated to protect.

The government is obligated to protect only those rights which the courts find are binding upon the government under the provisions of the Constitution, regardless of what is stated in the Declaration of Independence. People often make reference to statements about rights made in the Declaration when they feel that an injustice has been done to them. These appeals, if broad and persistent enough, may have some long range effect on interpretation by the courts as to what the Constitution means, but there is no legal basis for expecting the government to enforce directly any provisions of the Declaration.

FALLACY 17

The writers of the Constitution took care to include in it the primary principles of the Declaration of Independence.

The Declaration of Independence speaks of four main principles: the equality of mankind; unalienable rights of life, liberty, and the pursuit of happiness; consent of the governed; and the right of revolution. The original Constitution included none of these provisions.

First, the Constitution did not treat all persons as equal because it counted slaves as three-fifths of a person and guaranteed that slave importation would not be outlawed for at least twenty years. Second, neither the main body of the Constitution nor the subsequent Bill of Rights protects unalienable rights. The pursuit of happiness is no longer mentioned, and as provided in the Fifth Amendment you may be deprived of life, liberty, and property by the government so long as due process of law is respected. The idea of due process as a restraint on arbitrary governmental action is an important one, but it is far from guaranteeing unalienable rights which are not to be infringed upon at all.

Third, if consent of the governed were literally true, the principle would require that no governmental action would be valid unless those people it affected gave their willing consent to it. In effect this would in most situations require unanimous agreement before government could act, a very cumbersome and impractical situation. The writers of the Constitution were well aware of the practical problems of government. They agreed, therefore, that most decisions of government would require only a simple majority of 50 percent plus one, that some decisions would require an extraordinary majority of two-thirds or three-fourths, and that the ratification of the constitutional document would require approval by only a majority vote in each of three-fourths of the states.

Finally, while there is a constitutional right to alter or amend the Constitution, there is no right to abolish the government—no right to revolution. No American government is going to legalize the right of rebellion, regardless of what the Declaration of Independence might state.

Why are there differences between the Declaration of Independence and the Constitution? Basically each has a purpose which serves opposite political functions. The first is designed to justify revolution by stating principles believed in by those who signed it and by listing how those principles were being violated by the British. The Constitution, on the other hand, is designed to establish a workable government, not to justify the overthrow of one. Establishing a workable government not only requires some agreement on principle or style, but also calls for compromise to satisfy the different interests involved and the practical situation at hand. The requirements of practical operation, a problem all governments and human organizations must face, necessitated the modification of absolute principles into approximated goals.

FALLACY 18

The principles of the Declaration of Independence can be used to justify revolt only against a nondemocratic political system.

The principles of the Declaration of Independence are well suited to justify revolt against any political system in the world. No government, democratic or not, is capable of achieving the perfection required by the principles in the Declaration. When measured against these principles all political systems would fall short, even though we would expect that democracies would come closer than other systems in achieving the spirit, if not the letter, of the Declaration.

To those people who feel unjustly treated by government, the Declaration of Independence provides a convenient set of standards by which to measure the discrepancy between governmental practice and ideal. It is, therefore, often used as a rallying point for the discontented who hope to change the course of governmental policy, and for this purpose the Declaration serves a contemporary political function. This function is served not only for Americans who are desirous of equality or of greater liberty, but it also inspires oppressed people the world round, some of whom still view the American revolutionary experience as having meaning for their own plight.

FALLACY 19

Separation of powers is necessary in a democracy.

A system of government which provides for a separation of powers, in which overlapping authority to grant or withhold approval of policy is granted to two or more structures within the system, is not necessary in a democracy. Democracy only requires that *the primary governmental officials compete periodically for office in broadly based and freely competitive elections.* The particular method by which governmental decisions are made by these elected representatives is open to variation, so long as some public scrutiny of decision making can be obtained to facilitate holding elected representatives responsible for their actions.

Separation of powers, as established by the United States Constitution, is one of a multitude of political arrangements which is compatible with these requirements. Parliamentary systems which have a fusion of executive and legislative authority and no judicial review authority for the courts, such as in Great Britain or Sweden, can still maintain their democratic character. Executive leaders are chosen from among the majority party or coalition of the legislature which serves largely as a public forum for debate and questioning rather than as an independent structure of government which can veto policy decisions agreed upon by the executive officers. It should also be noted that separation of powers by itself will not ensure that the system is, or will remain, democratic. Many nondemocratic systems, for example, reach decisions through a process of policy consideration by several factions or special interests, each of which has a veto capability. The same could be said of some of the political machines or organizations which have controlled the political life of some of our states and major cities. In practice, this process of decision making by veto groups constitutes a separation of power, but does not produce democracy.

FALLACY 20

With their separation of powers idea, the concern of the Founders was to restrain both legislative and executive power, but not the popular will of the people.

Separation of powers gives each branch of government a separate constituency and the authority to veto or overrule the other. This system was intended to make it unlikely that one branch could dominate the others or rule alone. Instead, separation of powers makes it likely that there will be disagreement between the members of each branch as they try to represent constituency views. This system was designed to restrain all branches of the government, but it was designed especially to restrain the House of Representatives, originally the only one of the four primary structures of the national government whose members were directly elected by the people. The members of the other three structures were indirectly selected. Senators were chosen originally by state legislatures, the president was indirectly selected through an electoral college system designed to make independent decisions (which it no longer does), and members of the Supreme Court were, and are, appointed for life terms by presidential nomination and Senate confirmation. These branches or structures of government were designed, with their longer terms of office and indirect selection procedures, to act as a check on the House of Representatives. The members of the House, being directly elected for a two-year term, could not, it was believed, be trusted to act wisely because of close ties to the people. The popular or majority will of the people was, therefore, to be restrained, as were the various branches of government which could act as veto groups against one another by withholding approval on policy.

Having noted the intent of the Founders with respect to dispersing and balancing the decision-making powers of our national government, it should be noted that in practice the executive branch of government has come to play a very strong role in policy making through legislative initiative and budgetary coordination, and is almost unrestrained in the area of military and foreign policy. The executive decisions made to support our allies before December 1941, the decisions affecting our troop commitment to South Korea, and our involvement in Vietnam all illustrate this policy-making freedom. Whether this imbalance between Congress and the presidency continues or is reversed is still undetermined. It is clear, however, that institutional features such as separation of powers are not by themselves sufficient to maintain a check on the policy-making initiatives of a strong-willed president in historical situations conducive to policy innovation.

FALLACY 21

Separation of powers in American government protects our rights and liberties by preventing tyranny by either a minority or a majority.

These were the intentions of the writers of the Constitution, but in practice these results are not often achieved. Even if rights are protected it is still questionable whether it is a result of separation of powers or some other factor.

Since separation of powers acts as a check on the majority, it is sometimes difficult to enact legislation that might be approved by a majority of the population or of Congress. This is because members of the House and the Senate, and the chief executive, all represent different constituencies and have different terms of office. They therefore bring different points of view to bear on an issue. Under those conditions agreement is difficult. But history indicates that persistent majorities tend to have their way, delayed or not. There is little to suggest, either empirically from the historical record or in terms of logical necessity, that a delayed majority decision is necessarily a wiser one, or that justice is necessarily improved by creating obstacles for the coalition-building efforts of policy makers. This process impedes efficiency which in turn can impair the political system's capability to resolve current problems.

In one sense, a separation of powers does prevent a minority from tyrannizing by making it difficult to build a coalition to pass legislation. Separation of powers also permits persons or groups that feel unjustly treated to seek remedial action from a different branch of government if turned down in their first or second appeal for action. If Congress fails to act, perhaps the president by executive order can do something. If the Congress or president fails to act, perhaps the Court can deliver a favorable ruling. If the Court does not cooperate, perhaps Congress can initiate changes in the law or in the Constitution.

But in a very important sense, separation of powers facilitates minority tyranny by allowing the president or key individuals in Congress—primarily committee chairmen—to block legislation even though a congressional or popular majority think it wise for government to act. Presidential veto and initiative, congressional committee rejection of a bill, or the obstructionist tactics by committee chairmen constitute decisions made by one or a few, and allow a minority to determine governmental policy. This does not mean that such actions will always be contrary to the wishes of a majority of Congress or of the people, but we do not have to look beyond the recent history of the Vietnam war in the

1960's, civil rights legislation, or health care programs to find examples of minority tyranny facilitated by separation of powers. In each case public opinion polls revealed that a majority of the citizenry favored policy decisions that were blocked for a number of years by key figures in the administration or in one or the other branch of Congress.

It might be argued that the Supreme Court has acted to protect the rights of minorities, and this has been true at times. The court acted in the racial desegregation cases of the 1950s and 1960s; in the expansion of due process protection for both those arrested and criminally indicted; and for some of those minorities who sought the protection of the First Amendment for their religious practices or expressions of opinion. However, the Court has not always played this role. The Supreme Court has cooperated with the majority in the oppression of minorities: the Dred Scot decision denied citizenship rights to blacks; the *Plessy* v. *Ferguson* decision of 1896 upheld the constitutionality of racial segregation; the Court approved convictions of World War I protesters; and it sanctioned the incarceration of Japanese-Americans during World War II. As the Nixon Court comes to succeed the Warren Court it may once again become evident that what the Court giveth can also be taken away. This has been indicated by recent Court decisions initiating a constricting trend in regard to the due process rights of the accused in criminal procedures.

Because of the factors mentioned above, it seems doubtful that separation of powers functions in any consistent way to protect rights and liberties. If a majority overcomes the obstacles of separation of powers by constitutional amendment or the appointment of a new Supreme Court majority, there is no check on what it might do. If one branch is strong enough it may override the others and there is no effective check. If one branch or a minority group within government is able to block governmental action, a group of citizens might still be deprived of their rights by the actions of private individuals until the government can act to protect them. Therefore, separation of powers by itself is not sufficient, or even necessary or useful, for protecting rights and liberties from minority or majority tyranny.

FALLACY 22

If the checks and balances of our separation of powers lead to a deadlock so that no governmental policy is established, this means that no decision is made and therefore our liberties are protected.

This might be true if the decisions of government were the only source of infringement on our liberties. But throughout our history persons bankrupted by unfair business competition, jobless because of labor union or business discrimination, or persecuted or harassed for their religious beliefs have found that governmental action can also be expanded to secure the liberty to earn a living, practice religion, or engage in other activities. There is no guarantee, therefore, that governmental inaction protects liberty.

FALLACY 23

Federalism is necessary for democracy.

Federalism divides authority or jurisdiction for policy making between the national level of government and subordinate levels such as states, provinces, or regions. Federalism is used in many systems of government including the United States, Australia, Canada, and the Federal Republic of Germany. On the other hand, Denmark, France, Great Britain, Japan, Norway, and Sweden are some of those democracies with unitary systems of government having no federal divisions of jurisdiction for policy making, although there are among them varying degrees of decentralization for administrative policy making and implementation. From these examples we can see that federalism is not necessary for democracy but is compatible with it.

In large systems such as the United States, a federal system offers some advantages for dealing with the diversity of interests that makes universal policies difficult to apply and public participation difficult to maintain. However, federalism also permits local majorities to abuse and frustrate national programs designed to deal with national problems. This demonstrates the difficulty of *assuring* justice with structural innovations such as federalism.

FALLACY 24

State and local governments are "closer to the people" than the national government.

Geographically this is true; in daily importance it may be true; but psychologically it is not true. While it may be physically easy to travel to state or local seats of government, it does not necessarily follow as implied by the above statement that these governments are better governments; or that they are more responsive to the needs or under the control of all, or even a majority of the local citizenry.

It is true that many important decisions affecting the lives of people are made by state and local governments. Decisions concerning state sales and income taxes, local property taxes, police protection, public education, and various licensing and regulatory functions are made by the states and communities. National governmental decisions also affect people in important ways, ranging from the sacrifice of human life in war to the funding of domestic programs which determine tax loads and economic stability. Depending upon your situation and the issue, either national, state, or local governmental decisions can be more important in affecting your life by satisfying or responding to your needs. If you are of draft age, issues of war and peace may directly affect your life in a permanent way. If you are running a business, state and local licensing and regulation could be most important. If you are in the black minority seeking an equal chance to vote, buy a house, or obtain employment, the national government may be very important in providing equal opportunity.

It does not follow, therefore, that turning more functions over to state or local government will improve the quality of life for all, or for most, of those concerned. State and local government may not be responsive to individual needs if those needs concern decisions on foreign policy or interest rates. In many ways, state and local governments are subject to a greater misrepresentation of interests because of the many opportunities provided by small district size for malapportionment designed to favor one or another interest group, despite court rulings requiring election districts of equal population size. These units of government are also subject to the same follies, vices, and pressures as the national government, perhaps even more so. Well-financed special interest groups can usually exert more influence and dominate policy making at the state and local level than at the national level because the size and importance of these groups is much greater relative to the smaller units of government. One need only look at such groups as financial institutions, public utilities, manufacturers, farmers, and unions to recognize how great an impact these interests can have on national policies as well as on state and local governmental decisions. Firms such as General Motors, U.S. Steel, Standard Oil of New Jersey, Duke Power Company, and Burlington Industries have annual incomes that are greater than that of many state governments and most local governments. Given an equal amount of financial contributions and time expended, they are bound to have more impact on decision making by smaller units of government than on decisions made by larger units of government.

Psychologically, most people identify more closely with issues and representatives at the national level than at the state and local level. Few people can name the persons who represent them in the state legislature or in the county government, much less know what position they take on various issues. Many more people, however, know who their federal congressman and senators are, and have some idea of their stand on major issues. National issues take precedence over most state and local issues, partly because there is better news coverage of national political leaders and issues, and partly because people now have great mobility from one part of the country to another. The higher levels of interest and information concerning national affairs also tend to increase participation in national political activity. Voting data, for example, indicate that there is greater turnout for voting in national elections than in state and local elections. In terms of interest, information, identification, and participation then, the national government, not state and local government, is closer to the people.

FALLACY 25

The federal division of power or authority between national and state governments has increased the effectiveness of government in dealing with national problems.

Throughout our constitutional history there have been constant jurisdictional disputes about whether the national or state governments had the authority to take action on a given issue. Jurisdictional disputes are bound to come up in every federal system.

Since these disputes often take years to settle in the courts, or require a time-consuming and difficult process of constitutional amendment to settle the issue, some nationally important problems cannot be dealt with in an effective manner. Federalism has made it possible for states to take action on their own, and in some cases state action has been more advanced than national governmental policy. But the historical record also reveals years of delay in dealing adequately with national issues such as child labor in mills and mines, business monopoly or unfair competition, rights of the black minority, and labor's right to collective bargaining. Delay occurred even though a national majority was in favor of national action on these issues.

Federalism, at least in the United States, has not increased effectiveness in problem solving. Problems arise because conditions change over decades of time and produce situations having nationwide consequences, yet few if any precedents exist which can give jurisdictional guidance on the given problem. The current problem of air and water pollution is an example of a situation that now has consequences of national scope, and which will probably produce delay rather than action because of the policy evasions and disputes over governmental jurisdiction which federalism makes possible.

FALLACY 26

Debates about states rights usually reflect an interest in preserving constitutional principles rather than in protecting special interests.

Although it is difficult to make judgments about motives, it seems fair to say that those who argue in terms of the constitutional rights of states usually are doing so to protect a special interest or position which is protected by state government, either directly or by inaction. States rights is invoked when the national government threatens to regulate or control in favor of a different interest. States rights debates have been advanced on a variety of issues ranging from those arguments of New England merchants on tariff questions to southern stands on slavery and civil rights. There is usually an underlying similarity, however, in that the national government—backed by a national majority—wishes to take action contrary to the interests of one or several state or local governments—backed by a majority of local voters. In the civil rights controversies of the 1960s, for example, a national majority was in favor of the federal legislation that was passed, even though it was opposed by voting majorities in the southern states most affected by that legislation.

Whose will should prevail? The Constitution is not self-explanatory on this point, so generally the courts will decide. On rare occasions a constitutional amendment will be passed to settle the dispute. In the end, one or another interest or liberty will be protected or expanded, and the fight for protection of interests will shift to other grounds and techniques, leaving some other group to take up the banner for states rights.

FALLACY 27

Most innovations of the federal government in domestic legislation have been made in an attempt to solve problems that state governments have been willing and able to solve by themselves.

In terms of willingness to act, the record of the past century indicates that state governments were generally unwilling to deal adequately with the problems of an increasingly urban and industrialized society. As a majority of people came to live in urban areas and became engaged in nonagricultural work, state legislatures remained, in most cases, under the domination of rural interests. Failure to reapportion legislative districts to reflect population shifts to the cities increased the relative rural domination in legislation. As a result, in many cases, problems which became more acute in urbanized society such as care of the elderly, unemployment, industrial accidents, adequate housing, and social services were not dealt with because of unwillingness to be responsive to the needs of those affected.

Some states tried to deal with these problems but were unable to cope with them because of the costs and the competitive disadvantage involved. To meet the needs of those adversely affected by these social and economic problems usually requires expenditures of money by state governments or by business concerns. For example, if taxes are increased in one state, or businesses are required to contribute to an accident insurance fund, that state will be less attractive to business enterprises. Therefore, other things being equal, that state will be less able to compete with other states for business enterprises that produce income and tax revenue. Thus even if state governments are willing, they may be unable to deal with the problems they face until a federal program acts as a catalyst to enable all states to embark upon a new course at the same time.

Many federal programs have been adopted, therefore, because state governments have been unwilling or unable to act. Because of a somewhat greater responsiveness to urban interests, especially in the executive branch, the federal government has developed programs such as the social security system to help care for the elderly, unemployment compensation, workman's compensation for on-job injury, and interstate highway building projects. Given the past record of states, and the costs involved, we might expect much federal innovation and action, rather than state action, in dealing with the pollution problem. Such federal innovation does not necessarily mean that federal action is taken to the detriment of state government, because most federal programs require the cooperation and policy supervision of state government. To meet the requirements of the local situation, state agencies are given a role in planning and deciding upon the specifics of a general federal program. As a result of federal innovation and state cooperation, both the federal and the state levels of government have been growing in operational scope to meet the needs of a more urbanized and industrialized society.

FALLACY 28

Relatively, federal domestic budget expenditures have increased much more rapidly than state and local expenditures in the last twenty years.

Over the past two decades there has been a large increase in both state and local budgets and a rapid rise in indebtedness. The rate of state and local spending has increased more rapidly between 1950 and 1970 than federal government domestic spending. State and local expenditures have risen from $45 billion to about $130 billion while the total federal expenditure (administrative budget) rose from $46 billion to $155 billion. However, on domestic spending only between 1950 and 1969 the national government increased expenditures 219 percent, local government 364 percent, and state government 413 percent. (Governor Nelson A. Rockefeller in statement, January 1971.)

Much of the increase in spending at the state and local level has come about because of the rapid growth of urban and suburban areas after World War II and because of the need to compensate for the years of neglect in dealing with problems of urban and industrial growth. This change in responsiveness has been brought about in part by reapportionment of state legislatures to reduce the rural interest bias, and in part by a greater awareness of needs for a more equitable distribution of services in urban areas.

FALLACY 29

Most federal bureaucrats are employed in Washington in agencies administering social welfare programs and supervising the economy.

About 10 percent of federal civilian employees work in Washington, D.C. The rest are scattered among the 50 states and many foreign countries. Out of the total of approximately 3 million civilian employees (compared to about 10 million employed by state and local government) 42 percent are in the Department of Defense, 25 percent are Post Office employees, and 7 percent work for the Veterans Administration. This leaves about 25 percent to carry on all the other functions of the federal government embracing the ten other departments and 47 independent agencies. It could hardly be said, therefore, that the federal government is using most of its manpower in socio-economic administration and supervision.

FALLACY 30

The United States are governed as a republic, not as a democracy.

We are governed as both. There is no necessary relationship between being republican and being democratic. A republic is a nonmonarchical system which legitimatizes the government in the name of the people or by public involvement, rather than a system ruled by a king.

Democracy implies a system which reaches political decisions using the majority rule principle while protecting the right of minority opposition. Over the centuries from 400 B.C. the definition of democracy has changed from its original meaning of direct participation in the decisions of government by all citizens, to a more modern meaning involving a system of representative government in which competition for office becomes the key point of opposition and majority rule activity.

A republic could rely upon the democratic pattern of representative government as does the United States, or it could be nondemocratic as is the Union of Soviet Socialist Republics. A democracy, on the other hand, could be republican or it could be a constitutional, or limited, monarchy as are Great Britain and other West European countries.

In terms of currently accepted definitions the United States is both a republic and a democracy, although it is possible to be one and not the other.

FALLACY 31

Because of constitutionally guaranteed liberties in the United States, democratic rights cannot be voted away.

Constitutional provisions can be changed by amendment, and application of the constitution can be changed by statute or interpretation. During times of national stress (e.g., early 1800s, Civil War, World Wars I and II, anticommunism scares) many constitutionally guaranteed liberties have been violated. These included freedom of opposition, freedom of group membership, and freedom from arbitrary arrest and detention. If enough people approve of these kinds of restrictions and vote people into office who perpetuate them, it would not be long before democracy would cease to exist. Democracy thrives on peaceful opposition, but if fear of unorthodox or controversial ideas becomes too strong constitutional guarantees fall away.

The example of the Union of South Africa is a case in point. As the white elites in control of the system perceived what they thought to be a threat created by greater black participation in the society and government, they curtailed the right of open opposition and passed legislation which allowed persons thought to be politically dangerous to be detained without trial. In doing this the government became less democratic in its style of operation.

The United States has not approached the level of repression reached by South Africa, but there are indications that there exists a potential move in that direction. In 1970, for example, an omnibus anticrime bill for Washington, D.C. was pushed by the Nixon administration and passed by Congress which included authorization for preventive detention. This feature, it was argued, was needed to help curb the narcotics trade. The constitutionality of preventive detention has yet to be tested in the federal courts, but a precedent has been set which has ominous implications for political dissenters. Other recent indications of the potential for political repression were included in the results of a public opinion poll conducted by the Columbia Broadcasting System after a period of political dissent and unrest in 1970. The poll revealed that even if there was no clear danger of violence, it was thought by a 76 percent majority that political protests should not be allowed. A 55 percent majority agreed that the press should be prevented from covering stories that government spokesmen claim are sensitive in terms of national interest, even in a peacetime situation. These poll results reinforce the findings of other studies that have been made to determine the level of public commitment to democratic values.

There is no way to offset this potential for undermining democracy except by the determined efforts of people who respect the value of democratic liberties. They must convince the public and political leaders not to sacrifice too much freedom for the sake of system stability. But such warnings have no guarantee of success. The system can continue to operate, even though it may no longer be as democratic as it once was, because a political system can maintain itself without being democratic. A basic requisite of every system (political or otherwise) is stability, defined as persistence of pattern over time. Democracy, on the other hand, is not a system requisite, but a matter of style. It is a luxury to be added or achieved once stability is assured.

FALLACY 32

Constitutionally protected rights essential for American democracy include the right to bear arms.

In a country with a frontier and revolutionary tradition, such as our own, the right to bear arms for personal use becomes important in the minds of many men. As this view became embedded in the American culture it passed on to succeeding generations. The right to keep and bear arms is given a legal foundation by the Second Amendment to the Constitution. But it is usually conveniently ignored that this constitutional right is conditional; the condition being that the right of the people to keep and bear arms is related to the need for "a well-regulated Militia" which is "necessary to the security of a free State." Moreover, nothing in the

Second Amendment is said or implied about the right of sportsmen or gun collectors to keep and bear arms for personal pleasures or pursuits. The right exists only for the public purpose of participating in an organized military defense unit.

Regardless of popular beliefs or the interpretations given to the Second Amendment, the relationship between the right to bear arms and democracy, American or otherwise, is neither obvious nor conclusively demonstrated. It is true that the right of resistance to tyrannous government is an important element in the democratic tradition. Although the arming of the citizenry or the formation of a militia of citizen soldiers has been at times a restraining force on arbitrary governmental behavior, the necessary connection between an armed citizenry and democracy is not necessarily demonstrated for several reasons.

First, at a practical level the development of weapons technology has placed in the hands of modern government such vastly superior firepower and equipment that personal weapons become largely irrelevant in effective active resistance to government. Rifles and shotguns are no match for missiles, tanks, fighter-bombers, machine guns, and heavy artillery. At a time when the armies of the government were little better equipped than the citizenry, it might have made more sense. But today there is no contest.

Second, all political systems are shaped by the beliefs and expectations of the people who are affected by that system; especially by the beliefs and expectations of social and political elites. The survival of democracy depends, therefore, not on military pressure from below by the masses of armed people, but on the people's expectation and belief—especially of elites—that democratic rules of the game are good and should be observed and protected. The belief in these rules, rather than force, preserves democracy.

Third, democracy requires peaceful resolution of disputes through the free and open competition of ideas and the acceptance of majority decisions. To argue that democracy needs to be buttressed by the weapons of armed citizens is to deny the main premises of democracy. Democracy cannot rest on force or threats of force. If the system does not have the willing support of the overwhelming majority of its citizens, it will not long be democratic, regardless of the state of armed readiness of the people. Free and open debate on issues cannot be forced, nor can willing acceptance of decisions be easily compelled. People can be forced to obey, but a system which relies on that type of obedience is not democratic.

Finally, it might be asked, if small firearms are impotent against the superior firepower of modern armies, why have the Viet Cong in Vietnam been doing so well for so many years against the superior fire-power of the United States' military forces? The answer is in two parts. In such a situation there is obviously no room for democracy. Force and violence destroy democracy. Second, such a struggle illustrates the importance in guerrilla warfare of having support from the domestic population and some skill in tactics. In this situation comparatively little initial support is needed from outside sources, since a large share of the weapons originally used by the guerrillas can be captured from the enemy. In building domestic support, it greatly helps the guerrilla movements if the ruling elite can be shown to be supported by the men and supplies of foreign interventionists, as has been the case with the Japanese, French, and Americans in Vietnam. In other words, if a situation develops that a government deserves to be resisted by armed force, it is possible to do so, given the right conditions. But those conditions do not necessarily include the prior arming of the citizens. If armed resistance or guerrilla warfare is to be undertaken, therefore, it can be done with the arming of only a relatively few fighters who have the support of a larger segment of the population.

SELECTED REFERENCES FOR FURTHER STUDY

Bakal, Carl. *The Right to Bear Arms.* New York: McGraw-Hill, 1966.
This is a well-written journalistic account of the recent history of the use of privately owned firearms in the United States and of the many attempts to regulate their possession. The author explores the firearms mystique and cites a wide range of statistics and incidents in firearms use and abuse. This record is presented as justification for stricter control of the sale and possession of privately owned firearms.

Corwin, Edward S. *The Constitution and What it Means Today.* 12th ed. Princeton, N.J.: Princeton University Press, 1958.
Each edition of this standard and scholarly work updates constitutional interpretation in the light of the latest Supreme Court rulings. It also provides historical context for these interpretations and traces the evolution of contemporary meaning. The author notes the growth of presidential leadership and the fact that all three branches of government have become involved in law making.

Corwin, Edward S., and Peltason, J. W. *Understanding the Constitution.* 4th ed. New York: Holt, Rinehart and Winston, 1967.
This is a concise and easily readable survey of constitutional provisions and their contemporary meaning. Each provision or key phrase is examined in non-

technical language. In addition the book provides a brief but useful analysis of each section of the Declaration of Independence.

Dahl, Robert. *A Preface to Democratic Theory.* Chicago: University of Chicago Press, 1956.

The features of this book that are relevant for this chapter are Dahl's discussions of Madisonian democracy and its methods of controlling majority tyranny. Dahl concludes that external checks on majority rule, such as separation of powers, are really not relevant to solving the problem of one social group exercising its power over another. He also notes that the problem of government is not one of majorities versus minorities, but one of distinguishing government by a minority from government by minorities. Polyarchy would be descriptive of government by minorities seeking to influence policy decision in a freely competitive situation.

Earle, Valerie, ed. *Federalism: Infinite Variety in Theory and Practice.* Itasca, Ill.: F. E. Peacock, 1968.

The contributors to this volume bring a variety of views to the study of federalism. With respect to American federalism, there is some disagreement whether there was to be a sharp division of authority between the national and state governments. There is agreement, however, that the division has not remained fixed. The chapter written by the editor notes that the development of political communities in metropolitan areas is essential to make federalism work to solve the urban problems of the United States.

Elazar, Daniel. *American Federalism: A View from the States.* New York: Thomas Y. Crowell Co., 1966.

This analysis of federalism in the United States notes the growth and adaptation of the system to meet changing needs. In the course of this change Elazar sees no overwhelming trend toward centralization of function as some have argued, but rather he sees an increase in functions and capabilities at both the state and national level. All in all, Elazar argues, there is no good reason to conclude that federalism has not worked well in meeting the needs of all Americans. If an issue is lost at one governmental level, the federal system encourages an appeal at another level. He does not view the federal system as one which prevents or impedes the effective solution of national problems—even the civil rights problem.

Friedrich, Carl J. *Trends of Federalism in Theory and Practice.* New York: Praeger Publishers, 1968.

The analysis of federalism presented here attempts to discover the conditions under which a federal structure of government would be an acceptable way to deal with diversity within a nation or within a world region of nation-states. The author stresses the dynamic character of relationships within federal systems and relates the potential for change to a variety of factors such as nationalism, party system, social structure, and opposition patterns. Because these patterns of change will affect the federal system impact on policy output, Friedrich disagrees with Riker's view that federalism will benefit only certain minorities and not others. It is also noted that the distinction between federalism and decentralization is not as clear cut as it appears, and that unitary government is not necessarily centralized.

Goldwin, Robert A., ed. *A Nation of States: Essays on the American Federal System.* Chicago: Rand McNally & Co., 1963.

This collection of essays presents a variety of views on the federal system. Most of the seven essays argue for careful guarding of states rights as opposed to central authority, and support the intentions of the constitutional authors in using federalism as a means to control abuses of governmental power. However, they do not discuss at length how this works in practice. The issue of whether state governments are closer to the people is raised, with Morton Grodzins arguing against this view and James Jackson Kilpatrick stating the affirmative. Harry Jaffa is singular in his plea for a stronger national government as a means to better deal with major domestic problems, many of which affect the national security of the country.

Goldwin, Robert A., ed. *Left, Right, and Center: Essays on Liberalism and Conservatism in the United States.* Chicago: Rand McNally, 1965.

This is a collection of essays including one by Martin Diamond on constitutional safeguards. He argues that contrary to the opinion of others such as James MacGregor Burns in *The Deadlock of Democracy* Englewood Cliffs, N.J.: Prentice-Hall, 1962, there is no incompatibility between democracy and the auxiliary precautions of the Constitution embodied in separation of powers, federalism, judicial review, and bicameralism. Although he agrees with the framers of the Constitution that these structural features are indispensible means for securing the best elements of republican government, and that they do in fact secure them, he also admits that these features will be only a temporary restraint on a popular majority which may, in fact, be tyrannous or inept.

Hamilton, Alexander; Jay, John; and Madison, James. *The Federalist.* Edited by Benjamin Wright. Cambridge, Mass.: Harvard University Press, 1961.

This is the collection of essays written in support of the Constitution and urging its ratification. It offers a defense of the key features of the document, including separation of powers, federalism, and bicameralism. It clearly states the intent of those who wrote the Constitution to preserve liberty and justice. Subsequent events, however, must reveal whether or not, and to what degree, those intentions have in fact been fulfilled.

Lockard, Duane. *The Perverted Priorities of American Politics.* New York: Macmillan Co., 1971.

In discussing the problems of American politics, Lockard stresses the importance of the structure of the system, or the rules of the game, in determining who tends to benefit from the decisions of that system. He notes the frustrating effects presented by separation of powers, federalism, bicameralism, and judicial review when national problems arise that might best be dealt with by national government policy initiatives. He also notes that federalism is a mixed blessing which helps racists to further their policies, while also reducing the scale of government to permit more meaningful and direct participation by the people.

Riker, William H. *Federalism: Origin, Operation, Significance.* Boston: Little, Brown and Co., 1964.

Riker examines federalism in several countries to discover general features of its origin and purpose, institutional patterns, and net impact or significance of the system for those people living within a federal system. He raises the question of federalism in relation to freedom or liberty, and notes that the important question is "freedom for whom?" Federalism, in Riker's view, is a system that will favor special minorities within the total system. In the United States these minorities are big scale capitalists, landlords, and most of all, southern white racists. If one feels that these minorities should have special decision-making privileges, one should also, according to Riker, favor the federal system.

Schubert, Glendon A. *Judicial Policy-making.* Scott, Foresman and Co., 1965.

This study demonstrates that Supreme Court policies tend to reflect basic changes of policy by the other branches of government as well as the changes of opinion by the population at large. It also demonstrates that there is no guarantee that a particular set of values will be protected by a given structural feature or function, such as the judicial review function of the Supreme Court. Just because a political structure was intended to preserve a particular value or ideal does not mean that in practice, or over an extended period of time, such an intention will be realized.

Spitz, David. *Democracy and the Challenge of Power.* New York: Columbia University Press, 1958.

Control of abuses of power in society is the point at issue in this book. Spitz argues that control of governmental abuses of power is only one problem, and that control of other abuses of power in the social and economic realm is another. Governmental features such as separation of powers, federalism, and bicameralism do not solve the problem because a majority could still get its way in establishing policy, and a faction could block legislation or the implementation of policy at either the national or state level. Therefore, a social or economic abuse could be allowed to continue unchecked by governmental action. Abuses of power cannot be satisfactorily dealt with by institutional arrangements alone. Each abuse requires its own solution as the issue arises, facilitated by reason and the good will of the people working within the democratic process.

The following journal articles are part of the ongoing analysis of some of the topics examined in this chapter.

Farkas, Suzanne. "Federal Role in Urban Decentralization." *American Behavioral Scientist* 15 (Sept. 1971):15–35.

Levy, Frank, and Truman, Edwin M. "Toward a Rational Theory of Decentralization: Another View." *American Political Science Review* 65 (March 1971): 172–179.

May, Ronald J. "Decision-making and Stability in Federal Systems." *Canadian Journal of Political Science* 3 (March 1970):73–87.

Monsma, Stephen V. "Political Leaders and Democratic Values." *Public Opinion Quarterly* 35 (Fall 1971):350–57.

Rae, Douglas W. "Political Democracy as a Property of Political Institutions." *American Political Science Review* 65 (March 1971):111–19.

CHAPTER FOUR

Law, Justice, Liberty

FALLACY 33

The United States Constitution guarantees government by law rather than government by men.

Yes and no. This is one of those pat statements which hides as much as it reveals and is misleading if not correctly understood.

How to control the arbitrary decisions of political rulers has long been an historical problem in philosophical discussion. If political leaders are responsible to no one but themselves, only the threat of rebellion has much impact on setting limits to political decisions. If rulers are responsible to a god as in the divine right of Kings concept, they may be restrained by unusual sensitivity or conscience. But when they are not so restrained the idea that they ought to be restrained offers little comfort to those who suffer in the interim from unjust decisions.

Developing expectations that traditional practices and rights should be respected has been important in restraining arbitrary rulers. Sometimes these have been codified or written into a basic organizational instrument of government such as the American Constitution with its Bill of Rights. So long as there are expectations by both rulers and ruled that these rules should be respected, arbitrary decisions will be reduced in severity and number. This is the generally accepted view of the meaning expressed in the phrase "government by law rather than government by men." Men who rule or make official decisions should respect the rights and procedures that law requires.

This is fine as far as it goes. But some questions still remain. Who codifies the law in the first place? Who decides what the constitution will require in a specific instance? Obviously, if we discount divine intervention or inspiration, we conclude that men decide what the constitution will mean. Laws that govern nations do not write themselves. Consequently, the laws that are to govern men are not necessarily neutral or objective on all subjects, as a reading of the U.S. Constitution will reveal. Many compromises were made in the writing of that document, such as how to deal with the slave population, whether to have congressional representation based solely on population, and what powers the Congress and the president should have. Decisions on these and other subjects have vitally affected the operation and decisions of the system and the kind of justice that has prevailed.

Even assuming a neutral and objective constitution, the laws passed to implement specific provisions of the constitution are not put into effect by themselves. Men decide which laws will be passed and whether they are constitutional or not. Men also decide how they will interpret the law in specific cases that come before a court or an executive agency such as the Federal Trade Commission or the Department of Justice. In any particular situation it is useful to know what the law requires so that officials cannot make up laws as they go along. But specific as the law may be, it still leaves room for various interpretations when applied. Laws must be somewhat general in nature because they must apply to classes of cases or instances rather than to specific cases. Therefore, human judgment or discretion will play a part in most all cases of a legal nature. To say that we are governed by law rather than men is at best a half truth. It then follows by the rules of logic that any partly false statement of this kind is entirely false.

FALLACY 34

Fair and equitable law enforcement is assured by constitutional guarantees and the system of laws at all levels of government.

Law enforcement, as in any other government action, involves decisions by men. These men are sworn to uphold the law, but the law does not enforce itself. Men must decide how the law is applied, and often these men are in difficult situations requiring quick judgment. Constitutional rights of due process help to ensure that an accused person will be afforded certain procedural rights. Knowledge of the charges levied, access to legal counsel, and the right of appeal to higher courts are examples of procedural rights. However, the following are not infrequent occurrences: the arrest of people on frivolous charges; the summary punishment of people accused of resisting arrest; the setting of excessive bail if charged with an offense; the bargaining with the defendant, even if innocent, to reduce the charge to obtain a guilty plea; or the concealment from the defense of evidence which might aid in the defense of the accused.

Law enforcement generally reflects the expectations of the voting public in a city, state, or nation, and specifically reflects the conceptions of the law enforcement personnel as to what is or is not important. In every community, for example, there are laws on the books from times past that are entirely ignored or given token enforcement. Occasionally police powers are used for political purposes or to harass persons deemed to be political enemies. In addition, those persons or minorities who are disfavored by the public in general, or by law enforcement personnel in particular, can expect to receive special, and perhaps unfair, treatment. This is why: killers of civil rights workers have seldom been charged with violations of state laws against murder, although they have been convicted on federal charges of violating federal civil rights; youths who may use replicas of the American flag for decorations are arrested and charged with flag desecration (though convictions are seldom upheld on appeal), while movie stars or commercial firms are not charged for doing the same thing; or housing codes are enforced in some parts of town and not in others.

In other words, national, state, and local expectations of what is reasonable in terms of law enforcement, together with the role conceptions of law enforcement personnel, determine how justly and equitably the law is enforced, regardless of what the constitution or the law might say. Some state or local abuses may be corrected by appeal to higher courts at the state or federal level, but most often the sacrifice and cost endured while waiting for an appeal to remedy a situation is enough to allow an injustice to stand. The best remedy is an enlightened and aware public that will not tolerate discriminatory and unequal law enforcement. The law, itself, is a weak reed to lean upon unless supported by vigorous and fair-minded public opinion.

FALLACY 35

The many technicalities which permit criminals to go free are not a necessary part of our constitutional rights to due process of law.

In the first place, anyone who goes free because of a technicality is not a criminal, unless found guilty in a court of law. The presumption is that the suspect—a citizen (not yet a criminal)—is innocent until proven guilty in a legal proceeding that protects his right of due process. If an appeals court overturns a conviction because of a technical infringement of due process rights the defendant may be subject to a second trial to be conducted in the light of the appeals court ruling. Such was the case, for example, after the landmark decision of *Miranda* v. *Arizona* in which the conviction was overturned and the right to counsel was extended to pretrial procedures, but the defendant was retried on the same charge.

Second, due process of law is primarily a set of technicalities designed to safeguard the right of each citizen to fair treatment if charged with a law violation. These technicalities include the right of each individual to know the charges, to legal counsel, to protection from illegal search and seizure, to question witnesses, and to appeal a verdict. If these and other technicalities are taken away, due process of law has been removed.

These provisions of our legal system have developed in the British and American experience over several centuries to restrain arbitrary and capricious applications of the law and to provide the citizen with means of protection from enforcement officials who happen to be political enemies. These procedural safeguards are designed to ensure that, so far as humanly possible, justice will be done. If there is a bias in these safeguards it is in favor of the citizen. The assumption that generally prevails among guardians of due process of law is that given the frailties of human institutions, it is better if the rules of due process in our system of justice are such that no innocent persons are wrongly convicted and punished, even at the price of allowing a few guilty persons to go free.

FALLACY 36

Led by the Supreme Court with the power to declare laws unconstitutional (judicial review), the federal judiciary ensures that justice will prevail.

Judicial review ensures only that you can contest the constitutionality of state and federal law in the courts and argue your case. There is no assurance that your conception of justice will be upheld or that the courts will agree to include your case among the minority of cases accepted for appeal hearings. It provides another arena in which you may possibly pursue your view of justice.

Insofar as justice implies an absolute standard of right and wrong, or truth and falsehood, the courts are no more privy to the secrets of eternal truth than any other group of men. Insofar as justice entails reasonableness or equity in the light of historical and cultural circumstances, members of the court may be just as out of touch with these circumstances as are members of Congress or the executive. While the federal courts are designed to be removed from political pressure, in practice their decisions tend to reflect the political preferences of the judges on the bench, if not always the preferences of the president who appointed them. But they are also in a position to act independently of the popular passions of the moment, and may overturn an act of Congress or an executive order which appears to violate constitutional standards, as the Court interprets them. Again, however, there is no guarantee which side of the issue the Court will support.

Generally, the Supreme Court will follow or lag somewhat behind national policy and social trends. If your conception of justice is in accord with national trends rather than with state or local situations, it is more likely that judicial review by federal courts will promote your brand of justice. If your views are not in accord with national trends, then judicial review will not tend to promote your view of justice.

FALLACY 37

The phrases of the Constitution are written in a clear and straightforward style, and obviously mean what they say so that they need little interpretation by the courts.

The Constitution defines basic principles of government and allocates authority and restrictions among the major structures of the government. It does not spell out in detail all features or provisions of the legal system. It is a statement of principle, especially in terms of powers of government and individual rights, that is to be filled out in more detail by future legislation and interpretational refinement.

For example, it is not clear what is meant when Congress: is empowered "To regulate Commerce with foreign Nations, and among the several States"; can "provide for the common Defense and general Welfare of the United States"; can "make all Laws which shall be necessary and proper for carrying into Execution the foregoing Powers, and all other Powers vested by this Constitution in the Government of the United States, or in any Department or Officer." Can we clearly see when a person has been "deprived of life, liberty, or property, without due process of law"; or what is "unreasonable searches and seizures"; or what is "excessive bail" or "cruel and unusual punishments?"

These general provisions are important guidelines, but they need to be applied to specific cases in the light of current standards of reasonableness. The ducking stool and the pillory were considered reasonable punishments 200 years ago, but are not considered reasonable now. What was considered reasonable government action to provide for the general welfare in the nineteenth century may seem inadequate now. Tests of reasonableness are affected by historical experiences and the issues of specific cases. It should be clear, then, that the Constitution does not apply itself. In order to make constitutional provisions operative and more precise, it is necessary that judgments be made by Congress, the executive, and the courts.

FALLACY 38

The pledge of allegiance is correct in stating that we are "one nation, under God, indivisible, with liberty and justice for all."

Although stated as if it were an empirical reality, this is a statement of principle or of hope, that is to be approximated though never fully achieved in practice. If saying the pledge really rallies people to the challenge of improving liberty and justice for all—and not just improving their own interests—then such a statement is useful and rewarding. If, on the other hand, the recitation of this pledge leads people to accept it as an accomplished reality, it is better left unsaid.

To be "one nation" implies a psychological condition in which all people of a country identify themselves as members of a national community (American, British, French, etc.) and to be "indivisible" implies that everyone supports the political system as a whole. To a large extent these goals have been achieved in the United States, although there are significant minorities among some radical groups, black militants, and Indians who would rather be separate communities and neither identify with the American community nor support the existing political system. To claim to be "under God" is at best a presumptuous hope, and at worst a blasphemy. We may like to think that we have divine guidance in our national life and policy, and some wits have asserted that given the follies of our system such guidance has been necessary to get us as far as we are. To go beyond that, as some do in claiming divine purpose for our national policy, is to go over the brink of blasphemy by asserting, in effect, that the infallibility attributed to God is now an attribute of our government. This view, in turn, makes the normal political opposition and competition of democracy overly difficult if not impossible. Who is going to campaign against God?

To claim liberty and justice for all is at best a claim that the United States offers many opportunities for liberty and for the attainment of justice, though there is offered no absolute guarantee of either. At worst it is a claim that, if believed literally, becomes a cruel hoax on the many people who suffer injustices and deprivations of liberty—a condition that is a part of the daily lives of too many Americans.

FALLACY 39

Legal guarantees for freedom of speech and association and for periodic elections are sufficient to control abuses of power or authority by governmental officials.

These provisions certainly are useful for checking major attempts to abuse one's position of authority. Elections are held at fixed two or four year intervals and present an opportunity to pass judgment on past activities. But elections do not help, except indirectly, in exposing and controling abuses on a day to day basis. The right to speak out on abuses and organize against them will help, but there is always the problem of overcoming secrecy in government which prevents abuses from being exposed. A recurring governmental abuse of authority, for example, results from attempts by officials to gather information about citizens. Information such as that concerning income (for tax purposes) or census data (to determine population growth and characteristics) is gathered and used for specific governmental purposes that do not involve an abuse of authority—unless the information is used for purposes not intended by the law. Other data may be gathered secretly by the government, and this raises questions of invasion of privacy, especially if the data is not subject to scrutiny and correction by the individual concerned. Singularly pernicious is the compiling of secret dossiers detailing the political activities and beliefs of individuals. Such information often forms a basis for official harassment of persons holding controversial views, and constitutes a continuing threat to democratic principles. These principles require that people be free to speak out without being intimidated by threats of government action.

As yet there is no legal limit to the kind of information the government may collect. If governmental officials are prevented from abusing the information-gathering authority, it will result from the activities of concerned citizens who insist on corrective action as each abuse or threat of abuse becomes manifest.

The problem of public inertia or indifference is an impediment to this kind of action, and is especially troublesome if the right of free expression or association is at stake. Most people are not much interested in protecting constitutional rights unless they are themselves directly affected. Consequently, by themselves, democratic constitutional provisions are not sufficient to solve the problem. It is, instead, a matter requiring the efforts of alert and involved citizens who are willing to make the attempt to right wrongs and limit abuses in a never-ending process of social, political, and legal adjustment.

FALLACY 40

All laws are moral or just laws.

To assert that all laws are moral is to claim that the government is unable to make a moral mistake and enforce an immoral policy. It is to bestow an air of moral certitude and sanctity on laws which, in any political system, are made by fallible men and which usually result from political compromises based upon interests rather than moral considerations. In a democracy especially, the result is to remove or diminish the possibility of criticizing or opposing governmental policy, because to do so would imply a position critical of morality. Finally, it debases or denies the integrity of man by asserting that an officially endorsed moral position is superior to that of an individual, when the reverse could well be true. Government has enough ability to thwart individuality without claiming moral certainty for its laws.

Ideally, democracy permits people to believe what they will and to have the widest possible latitude in expressing political opinions. This means that expressed views of morality and justice will vary from person to person and from group to group. Public law and policy will tend to reflect the dominant or majority position on a variety of issues, but whatever that position is, it will be subject to criticism by those in a minority position. From the standpoint of political stability, it is useful to have everyone obey the law even though (or while) objecting to its content. However, from the standpoint of making adjustments in law or policy to better achieve justice, it is not useful to stress the moral perfection of existing law or policy. One could go beyond this to make a case, as some do, for disobeying laws that contradict one's moral position on a given issue, arguing that there is no moral duty to obey unjust or immoral laws. This question will not be dealt with here. Laws, and the governmental policies carried out through them, are useful and necessary in regulating the affairs of men, and it is expedient for men in most cases to obey the law. It is sufficient for our purposes to note that to go beyond expediency, and to insist on moral certitude for law or governmental policy, is to claim more for law than can reasonably be expected. Such a claim would also negate the impact of individual conscience on government, necessary in a democratic system.

FALLACY 41

One may decide to disobey a law deemed unjust because disobedience in this case is the legally correct thing to do.

The Declaration of Independence asserts the right of resistance to unjust laws and government to the point of rebellion against all laws and the total system enforcing them. An individual may find that a particular law violates his moral sensibilities, and after due consideration of the consequences of obedience versus disobedience he may decide to disobey that law. This may be the moral thing for him to do, and would not be incompatible with the values expressed in the Declaration of Independence. It would not be legal, however, because the Constitution does not recognize the legality or right of disobedience. Although a case can be made for not being punished for following one's moral principles, those who disobey a law deemed unjust can expect to be punished for their action.

FALLACY 42

There is little to distinguish, in their relationship to law, between those who violate the law while engaging in an act of civil disobedience and those who violate the law while engaging in other types of criminal behavior.

Civil disobedience is a political act resulting from moral commitment and personal despair over other methods of action. Most other types of criminal activity are motivated by hopes of selfish personal gain or results from rash and ill-considered behavior. Civil disobedience is not undertaken lightly. It is a prudent, specific action undertaken for specific larger purposes. There are at least four criteria for judging whether an act is one of civil disobedience. First, there must be a moral issue involved. The moral issue must involve a governmental policy or law that affects the lives of a number of people in a way that violates their ethical standards of judgment in the matter. Since civil disobedience is a *tactic* or *method* of arousing support for a moral cause when other methods have failed, it is likely that the ethical standards appealed to are more generally accepted by fellow countrymen who do not themselves engage in civil disobedience. The object of the tactic is to attract attention to the moral issue involved and to rally support for a change in the law or practice which will make it more just according to those standards. Robbing a bank, therefore, does not constitute civil disobedience even though the robbers may think the laws against such an action are unjust.

A second criterion is that those engaged in civil disobedience must give careful consideration to the consequences of their proposed action, and it is this point which raises some difficult empirical questions. But just as governmental policy makers or managers of any large organization must take risks and eventually make decisions—even though all the relevant facts about the consequences of their decisions are not available—so must those who contemplate deliberate violation of the law make a decision on the basis of available evidence—even if the evidence is incomplete or presents risks. Predicting the future is hazardous at best, but all of us at one time or another take calculated risks involving the future. Basically, from an individual moral standpoint, the judgment must be whether the consequences of continued obedience to the law are better or worse than the consequences of disobedience. If continued obedience appears worse, then the course of action becomes clear even if risks are involved.

If a decision to engage in civil disobedience is affirmed, the third criterion relates to how it is done. It must be done publicly and peacefully. If one is to arouse moral and political support for one's cause, then publicity and nonviolence are desired. Throwing a bomb into a church in the dead of night or overturning a school bus, then, are not acts of civil disobedience. Occasionally a nonviolent protest results in a violent occurrence because of reactions from those who oppose the protest. But if the protest was undertaken with nonviolent intent and all reasonable efforts were made to keep it nonviolent, then this criterion is satisfied.

Finally, those who violate the law must be willing to accept the legal punishment for so doing. There are some who argue that there is no moral reason for accepting punishment for violating an immoral law, but this then becomes a different issue and tactic, and not civil disobedience. Flight from the law to avoid prosecution is not part of civil disobedience. In fact, a conviction and an appeal of that conviction could be the way to dramatize the point and gain a ruling to invalidate the violated law and, possibly, the conviction. In this way a moral or just situation can hopefully be achieved.

These are the criteria that distinguish civil disobedience from other types of criminal behavior. This tactic is not guaranteed to work, and some people who doubt that we can achieve justice in our system believe it has few possibilities for bringing about change. Some moral dissenters are resorting to harsher methods of political protest. One of the necessary conditions for the political success of civil disobedience is that the goals desired by the protesters are generally compatible with the ethical standards of the population and political leaders. If this is not the case, such a protest becomes irrelevant to the immediate cause, even though it would demonstrate the indomitable spirit of man in the never-ending quest for individual integrity and social justice.

FALLACY 43

America has traditionally avoided violence in political and social disputes.

As Charles Tilly has stated in a recent book, what is notable about American history is not the violence that has been experienced in producing political and social change, but the willingness to forget this experience or deny its existence. Starting with the original skirmishes between settlers and Indians, we have had a long history of violence. The frontier fighting spirit and the desire for a ready weapon are still with us. Unlike the citizens of other countries of the world, most American men still feel that personal firearms are essential to life and living, even though many game animals are near extinction and there are no more frontiers to extend by force.

We should not forget that our country emerged as an independent nation in a violent rebellion. Americans extended frontiers by forceful conquest. Indian killing was a respectable activity from 1607 to 1890 when the final massacre of Indians occurred at Wounded Knee, South Dakota. The questions of the right of secession and slavery were settled by force of arms in the Civil War. The competition between growing business enterprises escalated to violence at times. Struggles between union organizers and business firms have had a long and violent history. The fact that almost 2,000 blacks were killed by Southern lynch mobs in the 20-year period from 1882 to 1903 is one indication that acts of violent repression against blacks were condoned and much more frequent than they are today. Riots in cities have occurred because of disputes involving taxes, draft laws, and racial animosity. Over 300 vigilante movements have, at various times and places in our history, accounted for dozens of deaths outside the law. The temperance movement was often embroiled in violent behavior. Feuds between families or groups have a long-standing tradition in this country. Compared to other democracies in the world the United States stands at the top of the list in numbers of political leaders assassinated since 1947, and near the top in the years since 1918. The data on assassination levels were presented in a staff report to the National Commission on the Causes and Prevention of Violence prepared by James F. Kirkham, Sheldon Levy, and William J. Crotty (*Assassination and Political Violence,* Washington, D.C.: U.S. Government Printing Office, 1969) as part of the effort to explain the high level of violent behavior in the United States.

Violent tactics may not solve problems in the most acceptable way. But that has not prevented the use of violent methods in this country in the past or in more recent times.

FALLACY 44

The basic cause of urban and campus riots in recent years has been the presence of outside agitators.

If this were true, it would not be a compliment to the leadership ability of those politicians and campus leaders who level the charge. No outsider is welcomed into a community as a leader unless local leaders are no longer respected because of their failure to meet the needs of the people. No outsider develops support for an issue unless a basis for grievances is already present. People are generally too apathetic to get involved unless an issue has become vital to them and it seems that little is being done by established leaders to solve the problem. It is very difficult to fabricate an issue out of thin air and to arouse people sufficiently to take any action on it.

Studies of the American people have shown repeatedly that most people like our political system and are willing to work within it. But this sense of legitimacy wears thin if the system output continually ignores the interests of particular groups or individuals. There must be some evidence that those in leadership roles are at least sympathetic if not responsive, otherwise conditions develop that result occasionally in small confrontations that could escalate into a disturbance of riotous proportions. We find that the charge "outside agitators" is usually heard when leaders who have been derelict in their duties try to bring charges of incitement to riot or conspiracy against the likeliest target. Occasionally such a charge is justified, but the record seems to indicate that most disturbances arising from political or social issues involve much more than that which can be blamed on one or a few outsiders.

FALLACY 45

Recent civil rights legislation and court decisions have eliminated all forms of discrimination against disadvantaged and minority groups.

Many laws enforcing discrimination on the basis of race, religion, or sex have been eliminated, but much remains to be done, especially in areas of education, employment opportunities, and housing. In some cases the law is difficult to apply because of the time and expense involved in undertaking a legal suit to challenge a discriminatory practice. It is especially difficult if the executive branch of government is lax or recalcitrant in pushing for the enforcement of existing court orders and statutory provisions. In other cases private or unwritten agreements and practices among union leaders, businessmen, real estate brokers, and educational leaders operate effectively to evade the spirit, if not the letter of the law. It will be a long and laborious process before women, blacks, and other disadvantaged groups gain the treatment they deserve under constitutional provisions of equal protection of the law.

FALLACY 46

Negroes can advance in American life just as other minority groups have in the past.

There are at least three reasons why Negroes face more difficulties in this country than other groups. First, there is the terrible legacy of slavery which condemned blacks to an inferior status from which many are still trying to recover. To succeed in our competitive system one needs a commitment to strive based upon a high evaluation of one's own capabilities, and evidence that many others in similar circumstances have succeeded. These bases for striving were and are seldom available for most blacks. For the male, it is helpful in the success syndrome if there is a strong family group which can be relied upon in times of stress—a group which has produced examples of the roles to be played for success. But another legacy of slavery has been that of a weak or female-dominated family structure which tends not to provide the male model of leadership which seems to be a requisite for advancing in our society. A recent Census Bureau survey reveals that 31.8 percent of the nation's black families were headed by women compared to 9.4 percent for white families. In 1960 the respective figures were 20.9 and 8.1 percent. The family structures of other minority groups have not had this problem, at least not to the same extent.

A second basic reason for different advancement records is the many years of legal discrimination against blacks, in both the North and South, which separated them out for inferior status treatment. Legal discrimination kept many blacks from obtaining the education and employment opportunities that other groups have been able to obtain and use as their stepping stones to social, economic, and political advancement.

A third reason, or roadblock, has been the persistent abhorrence of differences among people, despite the purported American ideal of tolerance and respect. As other groups developed into second and third generation Americans they tended to assimilate into the melting pot of American life, and they lost many characteristics that made them different, such as ethnic patterns of speech, dress, and mannerisms. But blacks do not merge that easily. Even though they may develop mainstream patterns of speech, dress, and mannerisms, they are still black. They are easy to distinguish, therefore, as members of a different group who can be sorted out for special treatment, and it seems easier for many people to do this than to deal with each person as an individual with specific qualifications.

To many people a man's blackness is more important than what kind of person he is or what qualifications he has to contribute to society. A person remains black even until the third or fourth generation of intermarriage with whites. There is a term, "octoroon," to denote a "person having one-eighth Negro ancestry," but no term to denote a person having one-eighth Caucasian ancestry. The implication, obviously, is that Negro ancestry is bad. Even if that ancestry is one-fourth, one-eighth, or one-sixteenth, there is something special about it that deserves special terminology for special categorization leading to special treatment.

The concept of racial difference is much overplayed, since differences between people within racial categories is much greater than differences between racial categories. It would seem logical, if for one reason or another people must be categorized by race (e.g., census purposes), that persons of one-half black and one-half white ancestry be allowed to choose which race they care to be identified with, since they are not clearly in either category. This same logic would require that persons with only one-fourth or one-eighth Negro ancestry be classified as white. Would the great tolerance and rationality of Americans be strained by this logical conclusion?

It should be clear at this point that black people in America have to overcome a set of obstacles that other groups have not had to face.

FALLACY 47

Laws cannot change attitudes.

Law can lead as well as follow public opinion by changing behavior patterns. If opinion can be defined as expressed attitudes, and the opinions expressed are honest reflections of attitudinal patterns, then studies have shown that an effective way to change attitudes is to change behavior. If behavior is changed, attitudes tend to change to conform to the implications of the behavior so that potential conflict is reduced between attitudes and behavior.

If an unjust situation is present, the impact is usually felt by the way people behave toward one another. If the law supports an unjust behavior pattern, there is every incentive to continue it, even among those who may agree that an injustice is being done. If the law is changed to support a different pattern of behavior, there will be an incentive to change behavior in that direction, especially if the law is in accord with the values, if not the practice, of the overwhelming majority of the people. Some change in behavior will occur even among those whose values are not in agreement with the legal change, since it is also reasonable to expect that most people will abide by the law. The new law, therefore, brings an immediate benefit to those who had been suffering the injustice. In addition, there is evidence that as people become accustomed to the new situation under the law they will adjust to it and even change attitudes concerning it, thereby making the change more pervasive over a longer period of time.

The civil rights field offers some instructive examples in attitude change. Despite opposition from both within and outside of the military, President Truman in 1948 issued an executive order desegregating the armed services. In a few years time there was almost total acceptance of the propriety of integrated military units. In regard to the use of public accommodations, the 1964 Civil Rights Act played a large role in gaining acceptance among segregationists opposed to the Act for the idea of desegregated facilities. Many fewer people today would support practices that require racially segregated waiting rooms at bus terminals or segregated lunch counters.

This does not mean that no problems will be encountered or that no opposition will arise. Few worthwhile changes are achieved without risk and effort. But to argue that it is better to wait for attitudes to change before an unjust situation can be dealt with by the law, is to ignore both the immediate benefits to be gained by the behavior changes brought about by compliance with the new law, and the long run gains of attitude change spurred on by the legal change.

FALLACY 48

That government is best which governs least.

If all governmental decisions affected everyone equally and laws were the only restraint on liberty, then this might be a valid assertion. Under such a condition, the fewer the laws and the less the government regulated our lives, the greater would be our liberties. But such is not the case. Although laws may be written in language that makes them applicable to general classes of events, governmental decisions usually affect people unequally, meaning that some people benefit more than others by most decisions of government. This situation arises because individual liberty is not an absolute, but is conditioned by the need to restrain liberty of action so as not to interfere with the liberties of others. Such restraint must be reciprocal for others if our freedom of choice is to be meaningful.

Many things can infringe on freedom of choice including the physical situation or possibilities, individual capabilities, access to information, social and religious custom, decisions in the economic or social realm, as well as governmental rules and regulations. Even if there were no laws, then, there would still be limitations on our liberty. One of the functions of law, especially in democracies, is to develop some ordered balance among the various restraints on individual choice so that no one person or group of persons is at an unreasonable disadvantage in making choices; in having opportunities for employment or business options; in exercising freedom in religious worship; or in satisfying other needs of daily life. Ultimately, every liberty implies a restraint to prevent others from interfering with the thoughts and actions of their fellow men. Such restraints could be individual conscience, religious belief, or pressure from social mores. But for such restraints to be effective, the sanction of law is required in many circumstances.

When laws are passed restraining certain practices by one group or type of individual, liberty is often increased for other groups or individuals. A law, for example, which defines some business practices as a restraint on trade, and therefore illegal, would increase the liberty of other businesses to function and survive on a more or less equal footing. A law restraining anti-union practices of business increases the liberty of union organization and action, just as legal restrictions on unions increases freedom of action for business firms or for individuals seeking employment requiring union membership. A national law or legal ruling restricting religious practices required by local governments increases the liberty of those not wishing to participate. It is not true, therefore, that every law reduces or restrains the liberty of everyone.

The adjustment of liberty and restraint is a never-ending process as new situations develop in the social or economic realm. Some restrictions on liberty which result can be removed without legal intervention. But others are not amenable to private resolution. People who feel unjustly restrained, therefore, will appeal for governmental action and may be successful in redressing the balance of liberty and restraint to their satisfaction, at least for the moment. In these situations that government which does not act—or governs least—could well be not the best, but the worst.

In a democratic system there is no ultimate judgment on what the final balance between liberties and restraints will be. At any point in time the balance will tend to reflect what most people find reasonable in the context of tradition, general or legal principles, and the circumstances at hand. The test of reasonableness as reflected by legislation and court decision in a democracy over a period of time will not guarantee perfect satisfaction to everyone. Some persons will feel unduly restrained, but the results will be better for most people, most of the time, than the decisions of a nondemocratic regime or the unrestrained decisions of private persons or groups in the social and economic spheres of life.

FALLACY 49

A law restraining business practices violates unalienable rights of liberty and property protected by our Constitution.

The Constitution guarantees no unalienable right to liberty or property. It guarantees, in terms of the Fifth Amendment, only that due process, as defined at the time, will be observed if the government chooses to deprive someone of liberty or of a property right. A law designed to prevent monopoly, anti-union practices, or pollution of water or air by business enterprises would not be in violation of any constitutionally guaranteed unalienable right. It may be judged to be in violation of the requirements of due process of law, but that is a different matter.

FALLACY 50

A law restraining a business practice must be justified in terms of the economic principles upon which our Constitution is based.

The Constitution is more or less neutral in terms of economic principles. It does speak of regulating commerce, borrowing and coining money, taxing and tariff powers, and protecting the obligation of contracts. These provisions do bias the system in the direction of a commercial economy, but within this broad context there is great latitude to use legislation and court decisions to structure an economic system in one or a combination of several directions; from mercantilism to socialism, from communalism to capitalism.

Regardless of the direction in which the economic system is structured by law, there would be little danger of violating any economic principles of the Constitution; only a danger of violating political or legal principles such as due process of law or equal protection of the law. If Congress and the president decided, therefore, to restrain a business practice such as traffic in hard drugs or monopoly tendencies in industry—or even to do away with the capitalist economic system in the United States—there would be no constitutional economic principles to prevent such a move. There would be only a test of reasonableness in terms of the legal principles of the Constitution.

FALLACY 51

Governmental regulation of business is always detrimental to the operation of the free enterprise system, in terms of its own principles, as indicated by the American experience.

A free enterprise system implies free access to several things including markets, labor, financial backing, and raw material or products. Such access may be impaired by monopoly tendencies of other businesses or labor unions; by collusion between business concerns or between business and labor; or by various forms of discrimination based upon a number of factors including race, religion, family connections, or the requirement of special treatment in return. Examples of all of these practices can be found in the American experience.

Legal regulation has often been employed to limit private restrictions on the operation of the free enterprise system. There are laws against monopoly, collusion, and other restraints on free trade, as well as laws against unreasonable discriminatory treatment of competitors or consumers. There are also agencies of government to aid businesses in securing labor and capital that they might not otherwise deservedly receive if left to their own resources. The history of the United States indicates that without these types of regulation and assistance, the free enterprise system would be neither as free nor as strong as it is at the present time.

FALLACY 52

A true free enterprise system existed in America only in the nineteenth century before the government started to interfere in economic matters with antitrust legislation in the 1890s, and with other policies in the twentieth century designed to guide the economy to certain economic and social goals.

The United States has never had a free enterprise system in which there was no governmental involvement in economic matters designed to attain politically defined, as opposed to economically defined, social and economic goals. Governmental policies have not been neutral, but have given aid and direction to our economy from the very first. Tariff and import laws were passed to aid infant industry. Federal and state assistance for building roads and canals aided the transportation of goods. Farmers were aided in the settlement of government owned lands, most directly by the Homestead Act of 1862 which gave each settler 160 acres of land in exchange for a promise to occupy it for at least five years. The railroad industry was given over 100 million acres of land between 1862 and 1866 to encourage westward expansion of rail lines.

All of these governmental actions, and others, subsidized the economic activity of private businessmen either directly or indirectly, and all of the policies were implemented to achieve what were viewed as desirable social or economic goals, such as the development of domestic industrial production or the settlement of western lands. Today there are also many subsidies to private business, including the farm price support programs, the oil depletion allowance, transport subsidies for airlines and ocean shipping, and the many government sponsored research and experimentation programs.

Governmental subsidies are seldom resisted by the business community on the grounds that they interfere with free enterprise, even though some businessmen and industries are favored over others. Government assists some corporations and activities to continue beyond the time when they can make a contribution to the economy or society on their own, such as Lockheed Corporation or the tobacco industry. Restrictions on economic activity are often opposed, however, on grounds that they interfere with free enterprise and violate traditional patterns of noninterference in economic activity. But if current efforts by government to achieve social and economic goals through regulation of industrial practices are opposed, it would more appropriately be done on the merits of the case and not in terms of a mythical nineteenth century ideal of governmental relationship to the economy.

FALLACY 53

Extensive governmental regulation of private property along socialist lines would violate property rights guaranteed by the Constitution and would mean that people could not own their own home or car.

The Constitution does not (as Justice Holmes noted in *Lochner* v. *New York*, 1905) implement any particular economic system, and it is compatible with several. Under present judicial interpretation of the Constitution, the government could legally enact legislation that would facilitate a planned economy and elements of public ownership of property that would be compatible with socialist economic theory and practice.

Socialism as applied by most West European democracies does not, however, necessarily imply governmental ownership of all income-producing property. In Sweden, for example, 90 percent of industrial employment is in privately owned concerns, about 4 percent is in cooperatively owned enterprises, with the remaining 6 percent in governmental corporations. The goal is the management of production and capital investment to insure conformity with long and short term economic and social goals as defined by publicly elected representatives. This is done on the assumption that it is not in the public interest to allow major producers to operate in a way that satisfies the self-defined interests of individual enterprises. It is believed that unregulated capitalism tends to produce distortions in satisfaction of needs, as well as periodic and painful rises and falls in economic cycles.

Socialist regulation or public ownership of property does not affect all property, but only income-producing property. Property which does not produce income (private homes, furniture, automobiles) is not involved in the public ownership scheme, and private property rights to these would be retained even if socialist guidelines were followed for public control of production.

FALLACY 54

Since values such as liberty and equality are so different, they are seldom in conflict.

These values are often in conflict because many policy decisions involve making a choice as to which one is emphasized or given priority. If the goal is a system of more equal access to health care facilities, for example, it may well involve some kind of public support or subsidy provided by tax revenue to those unable to obtain adequate medical services. But the tax revenue raised reduces the liberty of those taxed to spend their money as they see fit. A similar conflict arises in many areas of public policy. Equal opportunity in education may require desegregation of public schools in violation of some people's conception of liberty. Conversely, an expansion of liberty may require a sacrifice of equality, as in the business world, where freedom to combine into larger and larger units often reduces the chance for other firms to compete on an equal basis.

Much political conflict concerns disagreement about where the balance should be struck between liberty and equality in each of a variety of issue areas. Even though a decision is made on an issue, it usually does not permanently solve the problem of balance because various factions will continue to pursue the issue at other levels of government or in a different political structure.

FALLACY 55

Values such as liberty and equality seldom come into conflict if they are properly interpreted.

The problem here is the definition of proper interpretation. Who will decide what the proper interpretation will be? It well may be that illogical or biased interpretations of liberty or equality contribute to unnecessary political conflict. But even if these problems are solved there still remains the very great probability of conflict between these two goals (or others) that will not be resolved by clear and unbiased definition. Many policy decisions require a balancing of priorities involving several worthwhile goals. Here a choice must be made, and inevitably it requires placing emphasis on one or another value or goal.

Who will make such decisions? In a democracy these decisions tend to favor the stronger and more broadly based interests, though the choices seldom damage the position of the majority of social and political elites. The choice which seems reasonable at the time, given the values and priorities of those in a position to influence policy, tends to emerge as official policy concerning the proper interpretation or emphasis to be given to liberty and equality. As times and conditions change, interpretation and the policies pursued to reach the defined goals will change.

FALLACY 56

It is important for American democracy to have some limitations upon freedom of speech, because once the truth is known there is no useful reason to allow error to be advocated.

John Stuart Mill dealt eloquently with this question in his essay *On Liberty*. Some of his arguments can be briefly noted here. In the first place it is presumptuous to assert that any one person or group of persons should know what the truth is and to claim that other people are ignorant of truth. If this idea were to be given governmental sanction, it would mean that our leaders would develop an official truth immune from criticism. This would make it difficult, if not impossible, to develop the opposition and competition necessary for democracy.

Most visions of the truth are only partly true. If other views which may be partially true are outlawed, we would lose the benefit of improvements in understanding the truth. Even if there is agreement on what is true, it is useful for erroneous views to be advocated so that accepted truth is reexamined. These challenges to belief help to avoid the problem of people accepting things by mere prejudice without knowing why they believe as they do.

If all views are permitted to be freely expressed, there is a risk that the best or most truthful views may lose out. But not to run that risk is to make democracy impossible. Some faith is required that in the effective free market place of ideas, better alternatives will be developed over a period of time. If no good reasons can be put forward in support of an idea, then perhaps it deserves to be repudiated. Truth may not always win out, but unless the struggle between truth and error is allowed to continue, democracy as we know it will cease to exist.

FALLACY 57

In a democracy the freedom to express opinions of wide diversity and to organize to promote them should in all cases be limited to those who are of proven loyalty to the existing system.

Among the many political issues about which people disagree, is the question concerning whether the existing system ought to be altered in whole or in part. Persons believing that the system should be changed should have the right to speak out without having to prove their loyalty, unless we are to assume that the system is so perfect as to need no improvements. Those who wish an entirely new system should be allowed to gain as many converts as the persuasiveness of their arguments permits. If reasons for supporting the existing system are weak, perhaps the system should be altered or a new one established. To forbid the advocacy of some political views or the recruiting attempts of political organizations on grounds that they are being disloyal or un-American is immediately a sign of weakness. The use of force by the system to prohibit free expression is no sign of virtue for that system. In a democracy such prohibitions would require some compelling justification. But even if justified in an extreme situation, such actions would be an anomaly in a system that supposedly relies upon a free exchange of ideas as a basic premise of operation.

A justification for limiting free speech has been advanced by Harry Jaffa in *Conservative Papers,* (Ralph de Toledano and Karl Hess, eds. New York: Doubleday & Co., 1964) where it is argued that it is proper to discuss *how* to secure life and liberty of all, but not *whether* they shall be secured. No one has the right to advocate the latter, he argues, although it may be expedient to allow such advocacy if it offers no real threat to the security of the system. There appear to be two difficulties with this view. Although it may be an inherent right, as he argues, not to be proscribed or deprived of life or liberty, it is just as much an inherent right to hold and express the beliefs to which each human being is entitled as a mark of his individuality. To argue that only "civilized" views are permissible is to argue for some form of conformity which does not recognize individuality in its fullest sense. If man is to be free he must be free to hold the wrong views as well as the right views. As Mill has argued, the freedom to believe implies the freedom to express those beliefs. The conflict, then, is not between the inherent right not to be proscribed and a lesser right of opinion expression, but a conflict between these two as inherent rights for which there is no obvious solution to the problem of determining superiority.

The second difficulty has to do with the fact that most debates which result in actions that affect *whether* certain liberties are in fact secured for some, or for all, are carried on concerning *how* they may best be secured. The means used to affect the character of life and liberty usually become ends in themselves, even though the end result may not have been at issue. The debate whether to exchange freedom for slavery, which Jaffa would deny may rightfully be conducted, usually resolves into a question of whose freedom and whose slavery is at stake on a particular issue since all men cannot be equally free in everything. The problem then becomes not the relatively easy one of reducing the effectiveness of those arguing for slavery, but the more difficult one of determining the net result of various proposals for ordering or securing the various freedoms of a society.

FALLACY 58

The early settlers in America generally supported religious freedom and the separation of church and state.

The Pilgrims may have fled Europe to escape religious persecution, but many of them, upon arrival in America, set about establishing their own system of persecution based upon state religions. Matters of religious commitment and conformity were serious questions for most colonists, and the power of the state was often invoked to secure conformity. It was not until the early ninteenth century that the last state ceased to tax citizens to support the official state church denomination.

It was because of all the controversy and turmoil caused by official state religions that the first article of the Bill of Rights notes that "Congress shall make no law respecting an establishment of religion, or prohibiting the free exercise thereof; . . ." This kept the national government out of the usual religious controversies—but problems of definition are still with us today—while allowing the states to do as they pleased. This was so until the passage of the Fourteenth Amendment to the Constitution which opened the way for imposing national limitations on the states.

The relationship between church and state in America has never been consistent nor clearly defined and has undergone significant change in the last 300 years. There is little reason to expect change to cease on this issue in the future.

FALLACY 59

According to recent rulings of the Supreme Court, children may not legally pray in public schools.

Children may do all the praying they want to in public schools. The Court has ruled only that no officially sanctioned prayers (by teacher or school board) may be said in public schools. This position was taken by the Court on the assumption that such officially sanctioned prayers, even if nondenominational in character, lend the authority of the state to a point of view concerning religion. Since the state is neither to hinder nor promote religion, such prayers are unconstitutional. Studies of religion and the Bible are permitted, but only if a particular point of view is not promoted.

If any child feels the urge to pray in school, he has complete freedom to do so, so long as his prayers do not interfere with the studies of other children. If parents want a particular religious point of view taught, however, the Court requires that this be done outside of the public school.

FALLACY 60

America should promote Christian beliefs, because the foundation of democracy requires these beliefs.

If this is true, then the Jews in Israel, the Buddhists in Japan, the Hindus in India, and the Moslems in Tunisia are going to have a more difficult time than expected in establishing or maintaining their democracies. On the other hand, if Christian beliefs are promoted it does not mean that it will necessarily be supportive of democracy, since the historical record indicates Christian support for a variety of political systems. Princes and emperors have been supported by the Christian doctrine of the divine right of kings, and petty dictators and fascist rulers have gained Christian support based upon the New Testament principle of "obeying the powers that be," as found in Romans:13. Even in the American context Christianity has not always been supportive of democracy. Several colonies were governed more as theocracies under church rule than as democracies open to all faiths. Christian support for slavery was not conducive to achieving the democratic principle of political and legal equality for all.

The content of Christianity has varied widely over the centuries, especially as it relates to the political affairs of men. It is not necessarily true, either in theory or in practice, therefore, that good Christians make good democrats. Nor is it true that those who are good democrats are also Christian. Many value systems are compatible with democracy. Many leaders of our own country, including Abraham Lincoln and some of the Founders, have not been Christians in the usual sense of offering active support for a particular religious denomination. As long as the value or belief system is supportive of the idea that each individual is deserving of respect as an individual, and of its corollary that there should be political and legal equality for all men, then it is functional for democracy to promote such values and beliefs.

SELECTED REFERENCES FOR FURTHER STUDY

Abraham, Henry J. *Freedom and the Court: Civil Rights and Liberties in the United States.* New York: Oxford University Press, 1967.

This book stresses the importance of the court system in defining and strengthening the rights and liberties essential for democratic government. It also points out that, on a case by case basis, the courts are often involved in the drawing of a balance between individual liberties and the rights of the community. Constitutional phrases such as "due process of law" and concepts such as "clear and present danger" must be interpreted in the light of specific circumstances to achieve an appropriate balance. In comparison with other branches of the federal government, Abraham views the Supreme Court as better able to draw an acceptable line of balance because it is less susceptible to political pressure. In addition to due process and freedom of expression there are discussions of religious freedom and of equal rights for blacks in America.

Arnold, Thurman. *The Folklore of Capitalism.* New Haven: Yale University Press, 1937.

This exploration of the myths of capitalism examines how beliefs can suffer from cultural lag by not keeping up with practice or reality in terms of reasonable needs. It more specifically notes the discrepancy between beliefs about capitalism and the United States Constitution, and the practices actually followed by people in their economic and political activity. Arnold thinks that these discrepancies and outdated belief patterns impede the ability of the economy to operate at full productive capacity, and that they prevent effective governmental action to facilitate improvement in social and economic problem areas.

Buckley, William F., Jr., ed. *Did You Ever See a Dream Walking? American Conservative Thought in the Twentieth Century.* Indianapolis, Ind.: Bobbs-Merrill Co., 1970.

The views expressed in this collection of essays are, according to Buckley, representative of conservative thought and are concerned primarily with economic and political trends in this country, many of which are found by the contributors to be unwise, if not alarming. Among the positions supported are that unrestrained capitalism is essential for freedom, that individual liberty and order are the prime goals of politics, and that all the structural features of the government such as separation of powers, federalism, bicameralism are good.

Congressional Quarterly. *Civil Rights Progress Report 1970.* Washington, D.C.: *Congressional Quarterly,* 1971.

This volume is a collection of reports detailing a wide range of problems to be solved, and analyses of some successes in the civil rights field. Among the problems noted is that of weak enforcement of laws already on the books in such areas as discrimination in employment and desegregation of public schools. Also discussed is the suggestion by Nixon advisor Daniel Patrick Moynihan that the racial issue could benefit from a period of "benign neglect."

de Toledano, Ralph, and Hess, Karl, eds. *The Conservative Papers.* New York: Doubleday & Co., 1964.

Among the studies included in this volume are examinations of freedom of speech, and discussions which elaborate the meaning of conservatism and how it illuminates contemporary political and social problems.

Fortas, Abe. *Concerning Dissent and Civil Disobedience.* New York: New American Library, 1968.

In this book, former Supreme Court Justice Fortas attempts to emphasize the broad rights of dissent and protest which are protected by constitutional law, if not always in practice, and he urges Americans to respect these rights. He notes that there is a place for civil disobedience in our system, so long as it is civil and not violent, and so long as there are specific goals in mind which are possible to achieve within the general framework of the system. Only laws which are themselves believed to be unjust or immoral should be the target of civil disobedience.

Galbraith, John Kenneth. *The Affluent Society.* Boston: Houghton Mifflin Co., 1958.

Galbraith argues that the economic problem is no longer one of production shortages, but of the wise use of the abundance of our affluent society to meet social needs. The prime needs could be met, he asserts, by greater public expenditures for goods and services to meet those needs, together with diminished private consumption. The major governmental device to achieve this shift from the private to the public sector would be the use of fiscal policy decisions on taxing and spending, using governmental power as an instrument to reach goals that most Americans would find desirable and would support through the democratic process.

Goldwin, Robert A., ed. *Civil Disobedience: Essays Old and New.* Chicago: Rand McNally & Co., 1969.

This collection of essays ranges from Abraham Lincoln's espousal of a "political religion" to encourage obedience to law, to Henry David Thoreau's denial of any general duty to obey the law. It includes the defense of civil disobedience by Martin Luther King, Jr., and a rejection of that defense by Herbert J. Storing. It also offers some important distinctions between lawlessness and civil disobedience, as well as observations about general consequences of pursuing this avenue of dissent.

Goldwin, Robert A., ed. *Left, Right and Center: Essays on Liberalism and Conservatism in the United States.* Chicago: Rand McNally & Co., 1965.

The discussion by David Spitz is the most relevant part of the book for this section. He discusses the need to balance liberty with restraint, and the role of government as an instrument to effect an equitable balance of liberties for people in relation to that government and the spheres of social and economic power. In this view, governmental regulation can be a source of increased liberty for those who had been previously unduly restrained by the private decisions made by leaders of social institutions and economic organizations. Other contributors to the volume reject this instrumental view of government and offer supporting arguments for their position, premised mainly on the viewpoint that government is the primary, if not the only, source of restriction on liberty.

Goldwin, Robert A., ed. *100 Years of Emancipation.* Chicago Rand McNally & Co., 1963.

This collection of essays includes a range of views on the primary subject, in this case the status of the American black population. The views expressed range from those who advocate a do-it-yourself bootstrap approach, to the posing of the racial inferiority question, and to the presentation of the historical record of slavery and its consequences.

Graham, Hugh Davis, and Gurr, Ted Robert. *Violence in America: Historical and Comparative Perspectives.* New York: New American Library, 1969.

This was written as a report to the National Commission on the Causes and Prevention of Violence, June 1969. It is a collection of essays giving historical background to violence in Europe and America, and examinations of specific topics such as working class violence and racial aggression patterns.

Mill, John Stuart. *Essential Works.* Edited and with an introduction by Max Lerner. New York: Bantam Books, 1961.

In the famous essay *On Liberty* included in this volume Mill contends that the only rightful exercise of power over an individual against his will is to prevent harm to others. The use of such power is to be guided by the ethical standard of utility in terms of the "permanent interests of man as a progressive being." This would imply an absolute freedom of thought and sentiment; almost absolute freedom of expression; freedom of tastes; and freedom to organize for common purposes, all within the guidelines noted above.

National Advisory Commission on Civil Disorders. *Report.* Washington, D.C.: Government Printing Office, 1968.

This is the Kerner Commission's analysis of the racial disorders of 1967. It examines many facets of the problem, including the question of outside agitators, and makes recommendations for improving the general conditions existing in black communities to make violent outbreaks less likely in the future.

Shapiro, Martin. *Freedom of Speech: The Supreme Court and Judicial Review.* Englewood Cliffs, N.J.: Prentice-Hall, 1966.

In this examination of First Amendment freedoms and the Supreme Court, Shapiro notes that the Court can represent interests at the national level that may not be effective in gaining representation through the other branches of government. He also urges the Court to give a preferred position to freedom of speech, and shows how the clear-and-present-danger rule could implement this position.

Spitz, David. *The Liberal Ideal of Freedom.* Tucson: University of Arizona Press, 1964.

This collection of essays by Spitz includes several topics of relevance to this section. Among them are his discussions of the relation of liberty and restraint, the role of government in achieving justice or social improvement, the role of law in society, and a justification of civil disobedience.

Zinn, Howard. *Disobedience and Democracy: Nine Fallacies on Law and Order.* New York: Random House, 1968.

The nine fallacies that Zinn examines are drawn from the Fortas book cited above. He asserts that Fortas places too many limits upon those who would dissent from existing conditions and laws. Zinn argues for a broader view of what is justifiable resistance to law and authority in pursuit of justice.

The following journal articles are part of the ongoing analysis of some of the topics examined in this chapter.

Black, Earl. "Southern Governors and Political Change: Campaign Stances on Racial Segregation and Economic Development, 1950–69." *Journal of Politics* (33 Aug. 1971):703–34.

Marty, William R. "Nonviolence, Violence, and Reason." *Journal of Politics* 33 (Feb. 1971):3–24.

Palmore, Erdman, and Whittington, Frank J. "Differential Trends Toward Equality Between Whites and Nonwhites." *Social Forces,* 49 (Sept. 1970):108–17.

Peterson, David M. "Informal Norms and Police Practice: The Traffic Ticket Quota System." *Sociology and Social Research* 55 (April 1971):354–62.

Power, Paul F. "Civil Disobedience as Functional Opposition." *Journal of Politics* 34 (Feb. 1972):37–55.

Power, Paul F. "On Civil Disobedience in Recent American Democratic Thought." *American Political Science Review* 64 (March 1970):35–47.

Wechsler, Herbert. "Future of Political and Intellectual Freedom." *Virginia Quarterly Review* 46 (Summer 1970): 369–89.

White, D. M. "Negative Liberty." *Ethics* 80 (April 1970):185–204.

CHAPTER FIVE

Public Opinion, Representation, Interest Groups

FALLACY 61

Some governmental policies may be contrary to the opinions of the majority of the adult population in systems under authoritarian rule, but not in democratic systems.

Political leaders in democratic systems tend to be responsive to the desires of the majority, but these are not the only considerations involved in policy making. The majority may hold a view on some issue which elected officials think it wise to ignore. In doing so they will have to take the political risk of being defeated for reelection, but playing such a leadership role is attempted and is successful from time to time. The goal is to pursue the policy thought to be best, and hope that, before election time, a majority can be convinced of the soundness of that policy. This would be a proper way of proceeding and of playing the trusteeship role as a representative rather than a delegate role of representing majority opinion.

Another way to avoid following majority opinion is to operate in secrecy or by deception, a procedure which is more difficult in a democracy, but which nevertheless has an attraction for some politicians in all kinds of systems. This usually involves manipulation of events and public opinion to gain the desired policy goal, even though most people might object to the goal if they were aware of it. One could claim to be pursuing policy X which has some support, while actually pursuing policy Y which is unpopular. This tactic can be pursued in both foreign and domestic policy, as Americans have had occasion to experience from time to time.

In terms of foreign policy the Pentagon Papers revealed some of the secrecy and deception surrounding the U.S. involvement in Vietnam. Prior to the Tonkin Gulf incident in August 1964, for example, the United States had been involved in clandestine military attacks against North Vietnam since 1 February 1964 under the code name Operation

Plan 34A. But these provocations were not revealed to Congress as part of the situation which resulted in attacks upon two of our naval vessels off the North Vietnamese coast. The Tonkin Gulf Resolution was passed by both houses of Congress on August 7, therefore, with neither adequate knowledge of the situation to which the resolution was a response nor an adequate understanding of the executive plans already being implemented for an escalation of the war. Furthermore, these actions and plans were kept secret from the American public even though President Johnson was then campaigning for reelection by calling for "no wider war" in Vietnam. The situation was not much changed under the Nixon administration during which time a secret air war was being conducted in neighboring Laos, and the resumed bombing of North Vietnam was deceptively referred to as "protective reaction strikes."

FALLACY 62

In election years, as the campaign progresses, most people make up their minds on the basis of issues.

Most people have their minds made up before the campaign really gets underway, and their decisions may have little to do with the issues developed in the campaign. Studies of voting behavior reveal that people make voting choices for a variety of reasons, only one of which involves issues. People also make candidate choices on the basis of personality, and especially on the basis of their usual political party identification or preference. The dominant influence on voting choice will vary from period to period and election to election. But the low level of information which most people have about issues, or even about names of candidates, makes voting preference very often a matter of other factors, including the vague feeling that it is time for a change.

Campaign efforts seem to serve the function of developing enough enthusiasm and reinforced commitment so that the people who support a candidate will actually put forth the effort required to go out and vote. Considering the obstacles that make it difficult for many people to vote (bothersome registration procedures, working hour conflicts, transportation to the polls, baby sitting needs), this is no small task. In addition, campaign efforts can sometimes gain some votes from independent voters, or from the 5 to 10 percent who are undecided. In a close election, efforts to increase participation and change a few minds become crucial and more important than trying to change the minds of a majority of people in a short time span. Broad opinion changes usually do not occur as a result of the efforts made during the relatively brief period of a political campaign, but come about during the interelection period as people react to events day by day.

FALLACY 63

Independents, who do not identify themselves as supporters of any political party, are usually the best informed about the candidates and issues.

The image of the attentive, informed, and active political independent is a strong one in the United States. But those who identify with a political party tend to be more involved in politics and political issues. Studies such as those presented in the *American Voter* reveal that independents tend as a group to have no better knowledge of the issues than do partisans, a fainter image of the candidates, and less concern over the outcome of elections. It appears, then, that less involvement with organized political activity is *not* a sign of greater awareness, political sophistication, or civic mindedness.

FALLACY 64

The results of elections for political office demonstrate support for, or rejection of, a series of specific policy positions.

The outcome of an election demonstrates support for specific candidates for office, very seldom for specific issues. On the one hand, each candidate takes a position on a variety of issues, so how is he to know which issue people were thinking of when they voted for him? On the other hand, people may have voted for him on the basis of party loyalty or personality, rather than on the basis of positions taken on issues. Some may have voted for him even though they disagreed with some of his issue positions.

It is true that candidates and news reporters like to assert that they know what the election results mean in terms of issue support, but without some detailed polling of the public on a variety of specific issues, such claims to knowledge are simply guesses. The only voting results that precisely measure public opinion on specific issues are referenda votes in which voters can render a yes or no opinion on each item. But even these issue-focused votes do not reflect the opinion of all the people.

They reflect only the opinions of those who vote, and it is a common occurrence to have low participation (25–40 percent) in referenda votes even when they are conducted at general election time.

FALLACY 65

The results of public opinion polls carried by newspapers or announced by politicians are equally trustworthy (or suspect), even though different methods of collecting data on opinions have been used.

Opinion poll results differ widely in reliability because of differences in techniques used to obtain the data. There are at least two major problems which can impair the accuracy of results. First there is the problem of the loaded or biased question which biases the answer in a given direction. On the issue of busing school children to achieve racial desegregation, for example, one could ask, "Do you favor busing of school children to help them obtain equal protection of the law as guaranteed by the Constitution?" Or one could ask, "Do you favor busing of school children which takes them away from their neighborhood school?" The results would differ markedly. Yet questionnaires sent out by congressmen or local groups often contain biases of this type.

Even if the questions are not slanted in favor of one point of view, there is the second problem of ensuring that those people who respond to the questionnaire are representative of the area (universe) you are interested in, such as a city, a state, or the nation. If people are polled on the street corner or in a booth at a county fair or shopping center, or contacted by telephone in an unplanned way (all examples of a straw poll), the chances are excellent that the people polled will not be representative of the larger universe and the results of the poll will not be meaningful. If, however, those people polled are scientifically selected as representative of various social categories (race, religion, occupation, sex, education) in a *quota* sample, or selected so that every person has an equal chance of selection in a *random* sample, then the results could be reliably representative.

The major polls conducted by professionals, such as Gallup or Harris, attempt to use unbiased questions and scientific sample selection techniques. The results of these polls, and others using similar procedures, are accurate to within 2 or 3 percent. They are very useful for understanding what position is favored on issues, or which person is most popular as a candidate in an upcoming election.

FALLACY 66

Constitutional amendments, Supreme Court decisions, and recent legislation have eliminated all barriers to the exercise of the suffrage right.

Recent governmental decisions have greatly improved the opportunities for exercising the right to vote in state and national elections. This has been brought about by striking down legal restrictions which kept blacks from voting in primary and general elections, and by abolishing literacy or education requirements. These actions have aided many disadvantaged people of diverse backgrounds. In addition, positive action has been taken by the national government to aid in the registration of many blacks in the South who had been systematically excluded by arbitrary application of local registration requirements.

Despite these efforts all barriers to casting a ballot at election time have not been removed. In many states residence requirements are such that people who move about from state to state in our highly mobile society are often ineligible to register to vote for political offices in that state until they reside there for six months to a year. This, in spite of a recent Supreme Court ruling which struck down Tennessee's one year residency requirement and stated that a 30-day requirement for federal elections would be constitutionally adequate. In some states permanent registration rolls are not used and reregistration is required periodically. This results in loss of voting privilege for those who fail to reregister. Registration is often complicated by permitting registration for only a few days of the year, perhaps at a time sufficiently in advance of the election so that many people may easily forget to register. Too often registration dates and sites are not well publicized, and/or are deliberately made inconvenient for people in particular residential areas or occupations. At election time there is the problem of convenience or access to the polls in terms of both location and voting hours. Some polls open at 8 A.M. and close at 6 P.M., making it difficult for working people to vote. It is not unknown to find that economic reprisals and other actions are taken against some minority group members who dare to register and vote. Even though the law has helped, there are still barriers to exercising the suffrage right in the United States.

FALLACY 67

As long as the "one man, one vote" rule is followed there is little that can be done to favor one party over the other in drawing district lines.

One man, one vote ensures that each district will have the same number of people, thereby ensuring equal representation among districts. But this rule does nothing to ensure equal or fair representation within districts. If fair district representation is defined as a situation which is competitive in terms of enabling at least two political parties a somewhat equal chance of winning office in that district, then most state and congressional districts do not offer fair representation. In House of Representative districts, for example, only about 125 of the 435 seats are considered competitive, in the sense that winning margins are less than 10 percent (a narrower margin than 55–45 percent for winner and loser).

How do these noncompetitive districts originate even if they are of equal size in population? Within a state, in some cases there are broad trends in which most people are either Democrats or Republicans, making it difficult, if not impossible, to draw district lines that would ensure the inclusion of an approximately equal number of both. In many other cases, however, there is an approximate balance of party identification within a state, yet district representation tends to favor one party or the other. This arrangement, gerrymandered districts, can be established by guiding the drawing of district lines with an eye for partisan advantage. Take an example of a four-district area of 100,000 people, half of whom vote Democrat and half Republican. The four districts could be made highly competitive by including 12,500 supporters of each party in each district (illustration 1); or they could be made to favor one party three to one (illustration 2). Not only can one party be favored over another, but individual representatives can be favored or hindered by the redrawing of their district lines.

1
Competitive Situation
4 Districts—100,000 People

12,500 Dem. 12,500 Rep.	12,500 Dem. 12,500 Rep.
12,500 Dem. 12,500 Rep.	12,500 Dem. 12,500 Rep.

2
Noncompetitive Situation
4 Districts—100,000 People

20,000 Rep. 5,000 Dem.	15,000 Dem. 10,000 Rep.
15,000 Dem. 10,000 Rep.	15,000 Dem. 10,000 Rep.

Every ten years, after the census is completed, state legislatures, which are responsible for drawing boundaries for state legislative and congressional districts, become embroiled in political battles over apportionment. Members of both major parties are aware that whoever controls apportionment can also control the advantage in winning elections for the next decade, despite the one man, one vote provision.

FALLACY 68

Our elected officials represent the interests of all the people in their constituencies, whether district, state, or nation.

In a general way this is true; on some issues it may be true; but on most issues it is not true. Elected officials do represent the interests of all the people in giving some order to the affairs of government, and in articulating policy alternatives by which people can guide their choices at the next election. But most decisions on specific policy matters are going to satisfy some members of their constituency more than others, and some not at all. Representatives are elected, after all, with at least some semblance of competition between competing interests, and the winner can be expected to favor one group of interests more than others. Even if the district is a homogenous one with few differences to foster competition, there will most always be some opposition offered by citizens who do not feel that their views are represented.

Beyond this pattern of partiality is the fact that elected officials usually have little motive to represent the interests of people who do not vote at election time. If you are a member of an economic, racial, or social minority which does not vote in large numbers, the chances that your interests will be represented are very small, unless you have some other method of influencing election outcomes or policy decisions (strong group organization, wealth, access to publicity outlets). The probability is high, however, that if your group does not participate in elections at a high rate, it will not participate in these other ways either.

Politicians like to claim that they represent all the people, and this may be true in a legal and symbolic sense. When it comes down to whose interests are furthered and whose are frustrated, however, public officials do well to represent some of the people and not merely their own selfish interests.

FALLACY 69

The country would be better off if there were no pressure groups pushing for special advantage, since they serve no useful function in our democracy.

Pressure groups can distort public opinion to satisfy narrow interests, but they do nevertheless perform useful functions in a democracy. It might well be argued that one test of how free or democratic a country is depends upon how much freedom interest groups have to advance their policies. There are two primary functions performed by interest groups. First they arouse public opinion on various issues and bring it to bear on public policy during the interelection period. Elections provide the most direct popular control of representatives, but these occur only in two, four, or six year intervals, depending upon the office. Pressure group activity is not limited in this way and can be a means, therefore, for continuous public influence on policy.

The second primary function of pressure groups is to provide a forum for those minorities that are not well represented by the two major political parties. Since there are many interests or groupings of people that the political parties try to rally in support of their election efforts, it is often the case that some groups are left out, especially if they are small in voting number, are in a one-party state, or are not well enough organized to be able to guarantee most of their votes for one party or the other. These people can gain some representation in the political process only through a pressure group which speaks for them on policy matters, or brings cases to the courts in an attempt to protect their rights. Such activities are not guaranteed success, but these efforts provide at least the necessary basis for success and are a means for maintaining hope among the people they represent.

Pressure groups perform other functions as well. They can be a prime source of information on issues under consideration by governmental agencies and committees. Of course, if one point of view is not well organized or represented, a major problem can be magnified by pressure group activity and the information on which decisions are made can be distorted. Pressure groups also stimulate interest and participation in politics, and identify and clarify issues that help to determine election outcomes. Finally, pressure groups aid the legitimacy and, therefore, the stability of the political system, insofar as they provide a means of maintaining the hopes of the people whose interests they represent. Obviously, if an issue felt to be vital is ignored, it will be difficult to maintain this sense of legitimacy about the system among those rebuffed by policy makers.

FALLACY 70

The freedom to organize a pressure group to promote a point of view or to protect an interest ensures an equal opportunity to influence policy.

Freedom to organize is one thing; obtaining an equal chance to influence policy is an entirely different matter. Many organizations exist to promote and protect interests affected by public policy. But wide discrepancies exist between them in terms of political resources which might be useful to shape policy outcomes. Money, good organization, personal contact with decision makers, a favorable public image, and a large membership are all resources which can improve a group's opportunity to influence policy. These resources are not equally available to all segments of society, therefore those groups whose members are wealthy, socially acceptable, and in contact with key officials will have a higher probability of success. These characteristics mean that generally the most influential interest groups would be those whose members have prospered in the existing system and wish to protect their place in it; hence, they usually adopt a conservative stance on policy issues.

This does not mean that such groups will always gain their policy objectives or that policy making is always dominated by special interest groups. The American Medical Association (AMA), for example, is a wealthy, respected, and influential organization. Even though President Truman in the late 1940s had given support to the idea of federally assisted health care programs, the AMA was successful in preventing action on the matter until 1965. At that time the Medicare program was passed to assist the elderly in paying medical costs, and the Medicaid program of grants-in-aid to the states was initiated to assist needy persons not covered by Medicare. The AMA was powerful enough to delay action for almost 20 years, but fairly broad popular support for these health care measures, coupled with the Democratic landslide victory in 1964, finally carried the day against this interest group. Money, prestige, personal contacts, and support for the status quo give an organization an advantage in shaping public policy, but these resources do not endlessly guarantee success.

FALLACY 71

The government of the United States, unlike that of the Soviet Union, must try to meet the demands of a variety of groups and interests.

All modern governments, nondemocratic or democratic, must deal with factions and special interests. No man can rule alone without the assistance of at least a few others. These few others will have special interests to protect: various branches of the military, the police, civil servants, economic groups, or their own personal desires. Some rulers, such as Stalin or Hitler, have approached a situation of one-man rule in recent decades, but such a situation is almost impossible to achieve in large states, and certainly has not been achieved in the Soviet Union since Stalin's death in 1953. After the Cuban missile crisis in 1962, for example, Khrushchev had a very difficult time containing his own military leaders who wished to increase spending on weapons. This conflict, and other struggles among factions in top leadership positions, led to Khrushchev's fall from power in 1964.

There is certainly a vast difference in style between how the United States and the Soviet Union articulate and accommodate interests. Channels are much more open in the United States and participation in interest representation is much broader, especially through the competitive election process and activities of autonomous interest groups. But the difference in style should not cloud the fact that policy making in the Soviet Union, as in other large nondemocratic states, involves the same bargaining and special interest balancing.

SELECTED REFERENCES FOR FURTHER STUDY

Backstrom, Charles H., and Hursh, Gerald O. *Survey Research.* Evanston, Ill.: Northwestern University Press, 1963.

This is a basic handbook guide to the techniques of public-opinion research. It analyzes the problems in drawing samples, preparing questionnaires, and doing the field work necessary for reliable survey research.

Campbell, Angus, *et al. The American Voter.* New York: John Wiley & Sons, 1960.

Basic patterns and characteristics of American voters are revealed in this book. Among other things, it reveals the low information level of most voters and indicates which socio-economic factors play a role in determining political preference and behavior. It also demonstrates that a high level of continuity exists between elections, because over a period of years most people tend to vote for the same political party.

Congressional Quarterly. *Legislators and the Lobbyists.* Washington, D.C.: *Congressional Quarterly,* 1965.

This brief book gives a summary of lobby activity in the post World War II years, reviews lobby laws, and notes patterns of lobby activity in the executive, in Congress, and in the military. There are also four case studies, including one on AMA opposition to the idea of federal health care programs since the 1930s.

Dahl, Robert A. *Who Governs?* New Haven: Yale University Press, 1961.

This study of urban politics in New Haven brings into question the idea that politics is dominated by a political elite. Granted that there is an uneven distribution of political resources with which to influence policy, Dahl finds that the economic and social "Notables" do not always agree, and that they tend to specialize in areas of influence according to the issues involved. He characterizes this as pluralist policy making and notes that even if various interests form coalitions from time to time, they do not constitute a cohesive power elite.

Flanigan, William H. *Political Behavior of the American Electorate.* Boston: Allyn & Bacon, 1968.

Based upon data gathered at the Survey Research Center at the University of Michigan, this book examines several features of the American electorate including voting turnout, differences between partisans and independents, ideological commitment, and campaign impact. Flanigan's analysis reveals that independents are less concerned with election outcomes than partisans, but they are as interested in issues. No figures are directly available comparing information levels on issues, but it is inferred that attention and interest imply information. The low impact level of political campaigns is discussed, but he notes the difficulty of pinpointing opinion leadership patterns, although it is known that there is at least a two-step flow of communication from opinion elites through opinion leaders to passive participants.

Key, V. O. *Politics, Parties, and Pressure Groups.* 5th ed. New York: Thomas Y. Crowell Co., 1964.

A standard work on the role and activities of pressure groups, political parties, and political campaigns, this text has had several revised editions.

Key, V. O. *Public Opinion and American Democracy.* New York: Alfred A. Knopf, 1961.

This is an extended analysis of the distribution, properties, and formation of public opinion and its linkage to government. The book closes with a discussion of the value of popular participation in the political process and a call for responsible leadership if democracy is to survive.

Lane, Robert E., and Sears, David O. *Public Opinion.* Englewood Cliffs, N.J.: Prentice-Hall, 1964.

This brief volume examines the opinion formation process and explores the impact of family training, reference groups, and political leaders on this process. Also examined are the problems of low information levels, conformity, emotional intensity, and the difficulty of obtaining rational choice.

Milbrath, Lester W. *Political Participation: How and Why Do People Get Involved in Politics?* Chicago: Rand McNally & Co., 1965.

This is a collection and summarization of a range of empirical propositions which have been generated by a wide variety of studies to explain how and why people get involved in politics. The author outlines a hierarchy of participation extending from apathetics through spectator activities (voting), and transitional activities (attending a political meeting) to gladiatorial activities (being a candidate for office).

Milbrath, Lester W. *The Washington Lobbyists.* Chicago: Rand McNally & Co., 1963.

This study places lobbyists in the communications network of governmental decision making and examines a variety of patterns based upon interviews with a sample of 101 registered Washington lobbyists. Analyses are made of occupation patterns, types of contacts with government, and the role of lobbying in democracy. In general Milbrath concludes that little corruption is present in Washington lobbying, probably less than at the state level, although no evidence for the latter conclusion is offered. As a source which presents opposing viewpoints and information, lobbyists perform a useful function, even though the process might be wasteful and time-consuming. He concludes that the chief executive and the voters, in setting the broad outlines of policy, have a much greater impact on policy than lobbyists. Lobbying is no threat to American democracy, and well-informed citizens can keep it that way.

Mills, C. Wright. *The Power Elite.* New York: Oxford University Press, 1959.

Mills argues that a power elite consisting of those who head the hierarchies of state, corporation, and army are at the command posts of modern society. The elite are not only the possessors of power positions, but are also dominant in wealth and prestige which they use to shape policy. The backgrounds and training of these people, he argues, make their roles interchangeable and give them a coincidence of view and interest on major policy matters. He also argues that the power elite are not held in check by cultural values, nor are they held accountable by responsible political parties and elections, nor by a plurality of interest groups debating policy. Rather they have "succeeded within the American system of organized irresponsibility."

Salisbury, Robert H. ed. *Interest Group Politics in America.* New York: Harper & Row, 1970.

The topics covered by the contributors include discussions of interest group theory, the importance of organizational unity for effectiveness, and several case studies of interest group activity. The case studies include examinations of the National Federation of Independent Business, Students for a Democratic Society, Negro protest, farm lobbying, the AFL-CIO, and the political roles of the armed services. The book concludes with two chapters from the Milbrath volume which argue that lobbyists have small impact on policy and constitute no danger for American democracy.

Schattschneider, E. E. *The Semisovereign People: A Realist's View of Democracy.* New York: Holt, Rinehart & Winston, 1960.

Although the author views interest group activity as an essential part of the democratic process, he stresses that the pressure group system biases the influence pattern to the advantage of elites who tend to predominate in membership as well as in leadership positions of interest groups.

The following journal articles are part of the ongoing analysis of some of the topics examined in this chapter.

Boyd, Richard W. "Popular Control of Public Policy: A Normal Vote Analysis of the 1968 Election." *American Political Science Review* 66 (June 1972):429–49.

Converse, Philip E., *et al.* "Continuity and Change in American Politics: Parties and Issues in the 1968 Election." *American Political Science Review* 69 (December 1969):1083–105.

Curtis, Russell L. Jr., and Zurcher, Louis A., Jr. "Voluntary Associations and the Social Integration of the Poor." *Social Problems* 18 (Winter 1971):339–57.

Di Palma, Giuseppe. "Disaffection and Participation in Western Democracies: The Role of Political Oppositions." *Journal of Politics* 31 (Nov. 1969):984–1010.

Nie, Norman H., *et al.* "Social Structure and Political Participation: Developmental Relationships." *American Political Science Review* 63 (June & Sept. 1969):-361–78, 808–32.

Parenti, Michael. "Power and Pluralism: A View From the Bottom." *Journal of Politics* 32 (Aug. 1970):501–30.

Pomper, Gerald M. "From Confusion to Clarity: Issues and American Voters, 1956–1968." *American Political Science Review* 66 (June 1972):415–28.

Shannon, Wayne. "Electoral Margins and Voting Behavior in the House of Representatives: The Case of the Eighty-Sixth and Eighty-Seventh Congresses." *Journal of Politics* 30 (Nov. 1968):1028–45.

Wolman, Harold L., and Thomas, Norman C. "Black Interests, Black Groups, and Black Influence in the Federal Policy Process: the Cases of Housing and Education." *Journal of Politics* 32 (Nov. 1970):875–97.

CHAPTER SIX

The President, the Congress, the Courts

FALLACY 72

Separation of powers affords us three coequal branches of government.

The Constitution apportions authority among the branches of government in an attempt to achieve some kind of balance in affecting policy decisions. But it is very difficult to argue that as a result they are coequal branches of government. Throughout the nineteenth century it was generally agreed that Congress was the dominant branch. In the early twentieth century a number of Supreme Court vetos of congressional action in economic matters led some to charge that the Court was dominating policy.

In the past three or four decades most analysts would agree that the president has come to play a more prominent, if not a dominant, role in policy making. This is especially true in foreign policy where crucial decisions involving national commitment and even warfare have been undertaken with little, if any, prior congressional approval. Such was the case, for example, in decisions leading us into the Korean War and the Bay of Pigs action in 1961. It was true of our response to the Cuban missile crisis of 1962, our many stages of involvement in Vietnam, and our actions taken to improve relationships in the 1970s with the Soviet Union and the People's Republic of China.

It does not appear to be accurate, therefore, to speak of coequal branches of government. Depending upon the historical circumstances and the issues involved, one branch or the other tends to have a more prominent role in policy making. At the present time this role, especially in foreign policy, is played by the president.

FALLACY 73

Because of the guarantees of the Constitution, persons of demonstrated good character, leadership ability, and competence who meet the legal requirements for the office of president (age and citizenship) have a fairly equal chance at gaining the nomination and winning the election.

The inaccuracy of this statement is quickly revealed if one asks whether a person who meets these requirements has a fairly equal chance to become president, if the person is also female, black, Moslem, and poor. Beyond the legal requirements for political office there are many informal requirements or restrictions, especially for the Office of the President. Traditionally the informal requirements were that the prospect be a white, Anglo-Saxon, Protestant (WASP) and be either wealthy or have the prospects of raising a large campaign fund. These requirements have been modified somewhat in recent years, with the election of Roman Catholic John Kennedy, so that now one need only be a white Anglo-Saxon, Christian (WASC). There is some indication of further change as non-Anglo-Saxons, such as Spiro Agnew and Edmund Muskie, move closer to the possibility of someday becoming president. But even with these changes, informal requirements still leave out the person with any or all of the characteristics listed in the first sentence of this statement.

FALLACY 74

The presidential selection process (nomination and election) ensures that the person chosen is qualified and experienced in political leadership as a national executive office holder.

They may select a chief executive in Britain who meets these requirements, but not in the United States. Before a person becomes British prime minister he has proven himself as a national executive leader through many years in decision-making roles as an executive agency minister or cabinet officer. No one becomes a national political leader, much less prime minister, who has not had a long career as a politician.

In the United States, on the other hand, there is no clear-cut career route to the presidency. One popular route has been to become a military officer, and use the springboard of a war hero image to vault into national politics and the White House. Ten of thirty-eight presidents have been army officers, so this has not been an unproductive career pattern. Another popular route has been through a governor's office to the presidency, but this does not provide executive experience at the *national* level. In recent years the Senate has provided candidates for the office, but this background does not provide *executive* experience at the national level. The vice-presidency has also been a recent source of nominees, but vice-presidents are noted for their noninvolvement in high level executive decisions, participating even less than some cabinet officers and presidential advisors.

In effect Americans, when voting for a presidential candidate, take their chances of coming up with a capable man, a person who can make a satisfactory adjustment to the stresses and judgmental requirements of the office. Since presidential decisions are among the most consequential in the world, especially regarding peace and war in the years since 1945, thoughtful men are concerned that a better career pattern does not exist to ensure a greater likelihood that presidents will have adequate preparation for their demanding role. It is not enough to assert, as the pledge does, that we are "one nation, under God"; although it might be argued that given the career routes to top political offices in this country (through the military, a movie career, or as a pilot of space vehicles) we could not have gotten as far as we have without some sort of divine guidance.

FALLACY 75

Careful selection of rational men as policy advisors and cabinet officers will ensure the president of more agreement among advisors on policy priorities.

If rational men are also more willing to compromise differences, then agreement might more readily be reached. But rationality can just as well enhance the ability to defend a position as to promote prudent moderation. Cabinet members and advisors become committed to policy goals that are compatible with their political perspectives, or that tend to further the interests of the organizational structure to which they belong. Since these interests and goals often conflict there is likelihood of disagreement on policy advice.

In economic policy, for example, the Office of Budget and Management and the Treasury Department are interested in balancing the national budget as a goal. The Department of Labor is interested in securing full employment. The goal of the Department of Commerce is an expanding economy. The Treasury Department and the Federal Reserve Board are interested in ensuring price stability. Most of the time these four goals of a balanced budget, full employment, expanding economy, and price stability are simultaneously unobtainable. Too much price stability may prevent the economy from growing or full employment from being achieved. To spur the economy and achieve growth and full employment may require an unbalanced budget which spends more than is taken in through taxes, and which risks inflation and displeases those stressing price stability.

Because it is seldom possible to achieve each of the four goals at the same time, it becomes necessary to shift emphasis from one goal to another from time to time, requiring some agreement on priorities among advisors. Such agreement is hard to achieve, since policy goals of the various agencies change very little and each agency tends to feel that its goals should have top priority.

Policy advisors and cabinet officers have reasons for disagreeing on policy, therefore, even if they are all honorable and rational men. We should not think it unusual, then, if occasionally an advisor or cabinet officer resigns because of policy differences with colleagues or with the president. While in office they would have served a useful function by providing policy alternatives for presidential consideration. Upon resigning they can continue to articulate alternatives and play a more public role in the democratic decision-making process.

FALLACY 76

The Cabinet is the president's most important source of policy advice.

This may have been true in the nineteenth century. But as the Executive Office of the President assumed a larger role in policy making in the twentieth century and its size grew in numbers of employees and in functions performed, presidents have come to rely on a staff of personal advisors and assistants, most of whom occupy positions on the White House staff. In terms of personal relationships, political responsiveness, and political accountability, these men are closer to the president than members of the Cabinet.

Cabinet officers are often selected to satisfy political debts owed to various wings of the presidential party. In addition cabinet members are subject to the bureaucratic influence of the departments they head, and, unlike presidential assistants, they are subject to congressional control because of the budget and confirmation powers of Congress.

In this situation policy disagreement and even personal antagonism are more likely to develop between cabinet officers and the president. Such was the case, for example, when Interior Secretary Walter Hickel became critical of President Nixon in 1970 and resigned after policy disagreements and complaints of presidential inaccessibility to cabinet members.

Who controls accessibility to the president? Often it is members of the White House staff like Sherman Adams for Eisenhower, Theodore Sorensen for Kennedy, Bill Moyers for Johnson, and Harry Robbins (Bob) Haldeman for Nixon. These men perform a gatekeeping function and control accessibility to, and therefore influence upon, the president. White House advisors play independent roles in defining and advocating policy alternatives, as is most obvious in recent years in the realm of foreign policy. McGeorge Bundy, Walt Rostow, and Henry Kissinger have played very prominent roles in the administrations of Kennedy, Johnson, and Nixon.

The influence of White House advisors does not mean that cabinet members are always excluded from policy-making circles. It does mean, however, that with but a few exceptions, cabinet members tend to play a subordinate policy-making role. The exceptions tend to be relatives or close friends of the president, or they are persons of exceptional skills and dedication to presidential goals. Robert Kennedy and John Mitchell as Attorneys General fit into the first general category and Robert McNamara as Secretary of Defense for Kennedy and Johnson fits the second category.

Some have argued that the shift from cabinet advisory assistance to White House staff advice improves policy-making efficiency, coordination, and rationality. This is another interesting question. But there is little doubt that this shift in policy-making patterns has taken place.

FALLACY 77

The primary power of the president is his ability to rely on his position of authority to order people to carry out his decisions.

Very little that is important in politics gets done, except perhaps in foreign policy, merely because the president orders it done. There are at least two basic reasons why this is so. One is that the constitutional divisions of authority between the executive, legislative, and judicial branches of government permit presidential decisions to be vetoed by legislative and judicial decisions. The authority of these branches can counteract the authority of the president. The federal division of authority between the national government and state governments also enables state officials to effectively veto some executive decisions, despite the supremacy clause of the federal Constitution.

A second obstacle to presidential orders comes from within the federal executive branch itself. No man can rule alone. Even dictators require assistance from other men who are willing to help carry out national policies. The president is no dictator, but even if he were he would meet with resistance from lower levels of the administration; resistance resulting from a combination of inertia and policy opposition. On the one hand, there are those administrators who are involved in certain policy patterns and are reluctant to change, even though a new president is in office. On the other hand, there will be those administrators who in principle oppose some of the policy decisions of the new president and will do as little as possible to implement those decisions, so that the net result will be much the same as rejection. When a majority of lawyers in the Civil Rights Division of the Department of Justice signed a petition recently protesting Nixon's policies on civil rights, their numbers no doubt included both types of administrators. It might be said that the bureaucracy is the sustaining and continuing element of government, while the president is merely a temporary head of state with limited ability to effect policy changes.

Because of these obstacles to innovation and policy execution, the president cannot simply rely on the authority of his position to effect policy changes. Studies of the presidency have indicated that the most effective presidents are those who make careful assessments of the costs and benefits of pursuing various policy alternatives. They examine the bargaining resources at their disposal, and refrain from overcommitment on some policy issues which prevent them from having influence on other issues. Bargaining resources refer to the rewards a president can bestow on those willing to cooperate (which derive from the appointment and promotion powers, the access to publicity, the political campaign assistance, and the policy support which a president can promise or use) as well as to the deprivations a president can threaten by a contrary use of his resources. By prudent use of these bargaining resources a president can improve his chances of obtaining favorable action by Congress on his legislative proposals, and a more friendly reception of policy initiatives by his administrative subordinates.

FALLACY 78

The regulatory agencies of the federal government effectively control special interest groups and industries in terms of the public interest and safety.

Ideally, and actually at times, regulatory agencies of the government operate in such a manner that most observers would agree that the public interest or safety has been protected. Such would be the case if the Food and Drug Administration (FDA) prevented the sale of harmful drugs or mislabeled dangerous drugs; if the Interstate Commerce Commission (ICC) prohibited discriminatory freight charges; if the Federal Trade Commission (FTC) took action against fraudulent sales practices; or if the Bureau of Mines rigorously enforced mine safety standards to bring the accidental death rate down to the level in other industrial countries. But most observers would agree that this kind of action record in the public interest is not uniformly achieved.

Many instances of laxity can be found in the record of regulatory agencies. In 1969 a secret FDA report was made public which revealed that in the previous four years the FDA had recalled several hundred drugs because of mislabeling or defects discovered after the drugs had been available for sale to the public. The Bureau of Mines has been so notoriously lax in enforcing mine safety laws that in the 1970s the United States still has one of the poorest mine safety records in the world. The FTC was doing very little about deceptive advertising until a Ralph Nader investigation in 1968 and an American Bar Association study in 1969 inspired it to greater activity in this and other areas of its jurisdiction. In many instances the ICC considers itself a spokesman for, rather than a regulator of, the railroad industry.

These patterns of weak regulation arise for a number of reasons. Among them are the fact that over the years a government agency will develop close personal and professional ties with the industry it is supposed to regulate. Agency and industry members attend many of the same meetings and conferences, meet in official hearings and proceedings, have similar technical backgrounds, and at times change jobs so that industrial managers become regulators, and vice versa. However, another factor which contributes to weak regulation is political influence, either by tacit observance of the wishes of the governing party coalition and the president, or because of a series of politically inspired appointments to the regulatory agency over a number of years.

A perennial problem of government and bureaucracy is the difficulty of regulating the regulators. A new agency usually acts vigorously to achieve the intended goals of protecting the public interest. But over the years the public interest may be more difficult to define as conditions change, political considerations may become paramount, or an overlap of interest and personnel may develop between the agency and industry. It appears that most regulatory agencies need some kind of periodic examination, critique, and renewed dedication to original purpose. But this will not tend to happen unless the political context is suitable, and an aroused and informed public and reform-minded political leadership are willing to take the steps necessary to bring about the needed changes in personnel and policy direction. In this as in other areas of governmental activity, there is no automatic protection of rights or of what is conceived to be the public interest.

FALLACY 79

The legislative function is performed only by the legislative branch of government.

There are many sources of rules and regulations in most political systems, and the United States is no exception. Although the legislative branch of government has an important role to play in making rules for society in the form of statutory law, it is not alone in exercising this function, nor are statutory laws the only rules which govern the society.

The legislative branch is not alone in making statutory law because both the executive branch and the judiciary have veto authority—the president by not signing a bill and the Courts through judicial review. In addition, the primary source of legislative initiative is the executive branch which makes the initial proposals for most of the legislative decisions made by the Congress. This makes the executive branch an important part of the legislative process before and after Congress acts, and gives the executive an opportunity to shape the final outcome of legislation.

The courts are able to declare a statute unconstitutional through the judicial review authority, and can give more precise interpretive meaning to statutory law as cases are contested in the court system. In both situations the courts are able to say what the law is, or is not, thereby playing an important role in making rules for society. Just as congressmen must *interpret* the Constitution to determine what is constitutionally authorized in order to legislate, so Court justices in making their constitutional interpretations must *legislate,* in effect, even though the style and procedure of Court cases differs from the legislative process of Congress.

Another important source of rules for society is through executive orders and decisions. Some of these may be pursuant to constitutional authority vested in the president, while other rulings are made by the president or executive agency officers which follow the intent of statutory law. In either case, rules are made to meet specific circumstances which in effect are legislative acts, in the broad sense of making binding or court enforceable rules.

FALLACY 80

Congressmen usually consider only the preferences of a majority of people back home when deciding how to vote on a bill.

This may be what they say, but it is seldom what they do. Congressmen consider many things when deciding how to vote on a bill. Depending upon the issue at hand, they may be influenced by the views of their colleagues, by the outcome of compromises or bargains made with other congressmen or executive officers, by press reports and editorials, and by their own perceptions of what is preferable. In addition they may be influenced by their understanding of what a majority of people in their electoral constituency might prefer. Even if constituency preferences are thought to be of overriding importance on a particular issue, it is necessary, in political terms, to satisfy only enough people or interests to facilitate winning office in the next election. This means that only people interested in the issue need be satisfied, and then only if they can affect election outcomes in one of several ways; such as by comprising a large number of people who actually vote, or by demonstrating ability to influence election results through financial power, good organization, or other means.

If the congressman is deeply committed to a position on an issue which is contrary to that of his electoral constituency, he may choose to sacrifice his public career rather than compromise his principles. A few congressmen have taken this course. Those that have done so may well be included in a presentation of *Profiles in Courage* as examples of principled men who dared to advocate an unpopular view of justice. Such men, however, are seldom reelected to public office, nor do they become president.

FALLACY 81

One can easily tell what a congressman's position is on various issues by examining the voting records which are published by the candidates at election time.

Voting records can conceal as much as they reveal about the true issue position of congressmen. Several features of the legislative process make voting records difficult to interpret on face value alone. First, some crucial votes on legislation, especially in committees, are secret or unrecorded, yet the results of such votes cast by congressmen can vitally affect the content and success of a bill. Second, two yes votes on a bill may equal a no on the substance of a bill, where one of the yes votes is for an amendment which substantially reduces the effectiveness or changes the net effect of a bill. Third, a yes vote may equal a no vote when the yes is on a procedural vote which in effect kills the bill (a motion to refer the bill back to committee for further study). Given the work load and calendar scheduling of congressional committees, such a referral means that it is likely that the bill will not be voted out of committee again that session. Fourth, a vote on a bill may reflect the result of a bargain made with another congressman, rather than reflect a true position on an issue. Fifth, a yes vote on passage of a bill may be made with the understanding that provisions of the bill not desired by the congressman will be eliminated in conference committee meetings before the bill is voted on for final approval. Sixth, a vote on a bill may be cast in line with what is popular back home, but may not reflect the congressman's true position on that issue nor that of the party leadership. Yet such a vote does not upset the party leaders because the congressman casts his vote only with the assurance that his vote is not needed to gain the results desired by the leadership. Since the outcome of congressional votes is largely known by the leadership ahead of time, this is easily arranged.

For these reasons, it is difficult to rely simply on a yes or no voting record of a congressman to establish his real position on issues. Additional information is needed to clarify the context of the vote so that its meaning can be understood.

FALLACY 82

In the American political process the Constitution is interpreted or given meaning only by the Supreme Court.

Court decisions are an important source of interpretation, but they are not the only source. The general phrases of the Constitution are given meaning *directly* by most policy decisions of the government. This includes acts of Congress, executive orders, executive agency decisions, as well as a variety of judicial decisions at all levels of government. These decisions or official actions are assumed to be authorized by the Constitution and remain in effect unless challenged and reversed by an appeal body or court. If they remain in force, they help to define what the Constitution means in regard to the issue in question. They help, therefore, to interpret the Constitution.

Constitutional interpretation is aided *indirectly* from three sources. These include the proceedings of the original Constitutional Convention which provide insight into the intent of the authors regarding each provision; the analyses of constitutional law scholars in their writings in various law journals; and the long-range influence of well-argued dissenting opinions which are written as a minority view of a Supreme Court decision, but may become the majority view at a later time when a similar case comes before the Court. These indirect sources become points of argument or documentation used by attorneys, executive officers, and congressmen to justify the conclusions they have reached on the point at issue.

FALLACY 83

A Supreme Court with the authority of judicial review is necessary in a democracy.

The judicial review authority enables the Court to veto congressional or executive actions found to violate constitutional provisions. This authority may be compatible with democracy, but it is not necessary. Democracy requires a means for holding governmental officials responsible to the people, and open competitive elections provide that means. Democracy also requires respect for the rights of the minority to offer opposition so that elections are in fact competitive. It might be argued that the Supreme Court operates to guarantee that these minority opposition rights are protected. But there is no guarantee that the Courts will be any more sympathetic to these rights than are other branches of government. The record of the Court has been inconsistent in support of the right of political opposition.

In this century, for example, there has been Court support at times for (1) the 1917 Espionage Act under which antiwar dissenters were convicted, (2) the antisubversion legislation of the 1940s and 1950s (Smith Act, McCarran Act) where mere membership in the Communist party made one guilty of conspiracy to overthrow the government, and (3) the recent conspiracy laws which have been rather broadly defined and applied to curb antiwar dissent in the 1960s and 1970s. One can also note that the British have successfully retained their democratic character and rights of opposition without the aid of a supreme court with judicial review powers.

With the stress on constitutional rights in the United States (rather than a stress on reasonableness, fairness, or morality), the Supreme Court with its authority of judicial review serves a useful function in the American system. It provides a forum where differing conceptions of justice can be advanced in constitutional terms, and it produces legal opinions on these matters to help resolve political disputes. But in terms of democracy, it is not necessary that the Supreme Court play this role.

FALLACY 84

The courts interpret law in a consistent manner to settle disputes permanently.

Very little is consistent or permanent in politics, and this extends to court decisions. While court decisions are among the more consistent elements of governmental policy, they are subject to variation over periods of time, and to inconsistencies between various judicial districts, unless or until these are resolved by a higher court. Court justices cannot avoid applying their own values and perceptions to the issues brought before them, even though they are supposed to be impartial and removed from political pressure. The general phrasing of the Constitution, and of most statutory law, requires interpretation for application to specific situations. As conditions change the facts of a specific case will often require reexamination of the law in the light of the new situation to see if an altered interpretation of the law is required. These factors of individual perception, general phrasing, and changing conditions permit individual justices to find room for expression in their decisions, leading to inconsistencies between courts at any one point in time and to general change over periods of time.

Because court decisions become part of governmental policy, the decisions themselves can easily become political issues which lead to continued attempts to keep an issue alive by carrying the struggle into arenas of activity other than the courts. Our system of divided authority (separation of powers and federalism) offers many arenas of action for continuing a dispute as has been done, for example, with the civil rights issue. After the Supreme Court issued its rulings of 1954 and 1955, the desegregation issue continued to be fought in Congress, within the executive branch, at the state government level, by local school boards, and in cases brought again and again to the courts. There is little that is permanent concerning major political issues except the continuing struggles in and out of court.

SELECTED REFERENCES FOR FURTHER STUDY

Davidson, Roger H., *et al. Congress In Crisis: Politics and Congressional Reform.* Belmont, Calif.: Wadsworth Publishing Co., 1966.

The role of Congress in contemporary American politics is examined with a view toward examining alternative suggestions for reform. Three theories of

Congressional functions are discussed. Even though disagreement on function impedes reform efforts, it is noted that differences in concept of function are mostly differences of emphasis. Data on public and congressional views of Congress and its reform are presented. It is found that the least popular proposals among House members are the very items that most concern the outside critics.

The basic functions of Congress today are legitimization, policy clarification, oversight of bureaucratic activity, and constituent service. Major barriers to the performance of these functions include lack of information and complexity of decision making. The major goal of reform is to enable Congress to remain as pluralistic as possible so that the widest possible range of alternatives and criticisms are given a public forum.

Dexter, Lewis Anthony. *The Sociology and Politics of Congress.* Chicago: Rand McNally & Co., 1969.

Legislative policy making follows neither the pure democratic theory of direct instructions, nor the idea of pressure group dominance. Many factors influence Congressional voting, including role definition, salience of issues, political bargaining, and the congressman's sense of obligation to nation or constituency. Constituent contact is most often with those who agree with the congressman. In terms of public influence, Dexter agrees with Schattschneider that the people are semisovereign because neither elections nor interest group activity will determine policy outcomes over a range of issues for the benefit of a particular majority. The policy-making process is too complex to assure that any given priority or outcome will be determined by mass political action.

Froman, Lewis A., Jr. *Congressmen and Their Constituencies.* Chicago: Rand McNally & Co., 1963.

This is an examination of congressional election patterns, and of the relative effectiveness of constituency influence on congressional voting patterns.

Koenig, Louis W. *The Chief Executive.* New York: Harcourt Brace Jovanovich, 1964.

This is an extended analysis of the American presidency and its various functions, powers, and weaknesses. The author concludes that given the problem facing the American system in the last half of the twentieth century, there is a need for strong executive leadership, and that the foremost task of American politics is to convert the strong presidency "into an assured and constant feature of our government."

McConnell, Grant. *Private Power and American Democracy.* New York: Alfred A. Knopf, 1967.

This book examines the role of interest groups in shaping policy and argues that they are in great need of control and regulation if democracy is to be kept meaningful in the sense of keeping power responsible. Two-party competition helps control interests, but many states have weak party competition. Regulatory commissions of the federal government may help, but after a time they degenerate into maintaining the status quo and succumbing to the influence of those they regulate. Some way to preserve the public interest must be found. But this would require stronger central leadership and responsibility by the national government to counter the decentralizing tendencies of interest groups and congressional constituencies.

Neustadt, Richard E. *Presidential Power.* New York: John Wiley & Sons, 1960.

This is a guidebook for presidents who wish to maximize their ability to lead and exercise power. The author emphasizes the need to weigh cost against benefit in making decisions, and the importance of presidential persuasion for effective leadership.

Polsby, Nelson W. *Congress and the Presidency.* 2d ed. Englewood Cliffs, N.J.: Prentice-Hall, 1971.

A brief exploration of the American policy-making process as it is affected by a variety of relationships between Congress and the presidency.

Rossiter, Clinton. *The American Presidency.* New York: Harcourt Brace Jovanovich, 1956.

An historical examination of the presidency which indicates the various roles, styles, functions, and powers of that office as it has evolved over the years.

Rourke, Francis E., (ed.) *Bureaucratic Power in National Politics.* Boston: Little, Brown and Co., 1965.

This collection of essays explores several features and problems occasioned by the increasingly large decision-making role played by bureaucracy in American politics. Sources of bureaucratic power are found in expertise, information control, and support mobilization. Mobilization of public support for policies can result in a limiting of agency authority by inspiring opposition or by becoming a captive of the group that is mobilized in support. Efforts by the executive and Congress to control bureaucratic decisions can be effective, but the price is inefficiency. Efforts to remove politics from bureaucratic decision making appear doomed to failure. Attempts by Congress or the president to control bureaucratic power may depend not only on public awareness and supremacy of elected officials, but also on the ability to devise controls over administrative agencies that balance the ingenuity of bureaucrats to devise ways and means of escaping such controls.

Schubert, Glendon A. *The Judicial Mind: Attitudes and Ideals of Supreme Court Justices, 1946–1963.* Evanston, Ill.: Northwestern University Press, 1965.

This is an empirical study of the Supreme Court and how judicial attitudes affect policy-making in our government. Schubert's book *Judicial Policy-making,* noted in an earlier section, is also a useful reference book for this section.

Scott, Andrew M., and Hunt, Margaret A. *Congress and Lobbies: Image and Reality.* Chapel Hill: University of North Carolina Press, 1965.

Based upon interviews with a sample of 34 members of the House of Representatives, this study concludes that from the congressman's point of view, interest groups are only one of several influences shaping voting behavior. The congressmen felt that the most highly rated function performed by interest groups was that of providing information. But the information function is a weak basis of power, because it is subject to the channels provided by Congress and limited by competing sources of information. Freedom of action by congressmen is rather high in most issue areas. The primary limitation appears to be the degree of salience of issues in the congressional constituency. High salience coupled with active interest group involvement can be important in shaping congressional voting.

Sorensen, Theodore C. *Decision-making in the White House.* New York: Columbia University Press, 1963.

A brief analysis of presidential decision making based upon the author's experience within the Kennedy administration. He notes some of the limits upon presidential decision making, including the problem of gathering adequate and reliable advice from cabinet members and other advisors.

Wolfinger, Raymond E. *Readings in American Political Behavior.* Englewood Cliffs, N.J.: Prentice-Hall, 1966.

This is a collection of empirical studies focusing on Congress, the presidency, and the Supreme Court. It includes analyses of congressional voting and role behavior, presidential persuasion in the policy process, and the role of Court decisions in national policy making. There are also several case studies of decision making in each of these areas.

The following journal articles are part of the ongoing analysis of some of the topics examined in this chapter.

Adamany, David W. "The Party Variable in Judges' Voting: Conceptual Notes and a Case Study." *American Political Science Review* 63 (March 1969):57–73.

Boynton, G. R., Patterson, Samuel C., and Hedlund, Ronald D. "The Missing Links in Legislative Politics: Attentive Constituents." *Journal of Politics* 31 (Aug. 1969):700–21.

Clotfelter, James. "Senate Voting and Constituency Stake in Defense Spending." *Journal of Politics* 32 (Nov. 1970):979–83.

Downing, Rondal G. "Judicial Ethics and the Political Role of the Courts." *Law and Contemporary Problems* 35 (1970):94–107.

Grath, Alexander J. "Britain and America: Some Requisites of Executive Leadership Compared." *Political Science Quarterly* 85 (June 1970):217–39.

Prewitt, Kenneth, and Eulau, Heinz. "Social Bias in Leadership Selection, Political Recruitment, and Electoral Context." *Journal of Politics* 33 (May 1971): 293–315.

CHAPTER SEVEN

Public Policy: General Welfare and the Common Defense

FALLACY 85

The tax load in the United States is the highest among industrialized countries of the Western world.

The tax load in the United States has been averaging about 29 or 30 percent of the gross national product (GNP). This is similar to the tax load in Belgium, Canada, Denmark, Italy, and New Zealand. This level of taxation is smaller, however, than that in Austria, France, Great Britain, the Netherlands, Norway, Sweden, and West Germany. In this group taxes vary from 33 to 41 percent of the GNP. It would take an increase of more than one-third to bring the tax load of the United States up to the highest current level among industrialized countries. Such an increase would provide funds for many types of programs not now financed by the government. If some additional programs are deemed necessary to help satisfy various goals or priorities, there would seem to be little problem in financing them through greater tax revenues in terms of ability to pay the higher taxes. The primary obstacle would seem to be lack of willingness to pay, a matter of persuasion and commitment to policy goals.

FALLACY 86

The tax load in the United States is biased very strongly against high incomes.

The federal tax on personal income is at present graduated from 0 to 70 percent, depending upon level of taxable income. For a single person in the 1970 tax year, the 70 percent taxation level was reached when taxable income exceeded $100,000 annually. Such tax rates have been called confiscatory, and they may well be. The graduated tax rate becomes progressively higher on the assumption that those with the higher incomes should carry a progressively higher share of the tax load.

But analysis of tax loads in this country indicates that few people actually pay taxes at the higher percentage rates. For one thing, high income persons can avail themselves of a wide variety of exemptions, deductions, and special tax rates so that net taxable income can be made much lower than gross income. These possibilities for reducing net income levels permit about 100 millionaires each year to avoid paying any federal income tax. When the federal income tax load is combined with nonprogressive tax levies of state and local governments (in sales, excise, and property taxes) we find that the average tax load of the rich who pay taxes is not much greater than the tax load of the poor.

An interesting study by Melville J. Ulmer illustrates how the tax load was distributed in 1965 by level of family income (Table 1). It shows that there is no pattern of progression up to incomes of $15,000. It also indicates that the richest 10 percent (those families with annual income over $15,000) pay only 15 percent more in taxes, on the average, than families living below the poverty threshhold (most estimates place the poverty threshhold at $3,600 annually for a family of four).

TABLE 1
FEDERAL, STATE, AND LOCAL TAXES AS PERCENTAGE OF TOTAL FAMILY INCOME

Family Income	*Percentages*
Under $2,000	28.1
$2,000 – 2,999	26.7
3,000 – 3,999	29.7
4,000 – 4,999	29.1
5,000 – 5,999	29.4
6,000 – 7,499	28.5
7,500 – 9,999	28.5
10,000 – 14,999	30.6
15,000 and Over	44.0
All Classes	30.4

SOURCE: Tax Foundation, Inc.

These tax load figures are based upon reported income. Much earned income, however, is unreported and therefore untaxed. This untaxed income is not included in the figures above and makes the rax rate appear higher than it actually is, especially for those with incomes over $15,000 annually. A study by Glenn D. Morrow in the *National Tax Journal*

(September 1963) found that income from sources other than wages and salaries tends to be understated by about 33 percent in income tax returns. The net result for the tax load is summed up nicely by Ulmer:

> In theory the income tax should bear equally on people with equal incomes. In practice a great deal depends on how the income is earned. Those who live primarily on wages and salaries pay the nominal rates, literally and fully, in virtually all instances. The withholding and reporting systems of the Internal Revenue Service make any other result all but impossible. But those with incomes derived in substantial part from profits, rent, interest, fees, capital gains, and dividends—are able in a variety of ways to avoid a portion of the income tax to which they would nominally be subject. Since the latter types of payments accrue in significant amount almost exclusively to the relatively wealthy the progressiveness of the income tax is much more modest in practice than in theory.

FALLACY 87

Because Social Security taxes are not used to build up a fund for each person paying the tax, unlike private insurance or annuity plans, there is little to guarantee that contributors will receive payments when they retire.

As Benjamin Franklin noted, nothing is a certainty but death and taxes. But he and others had great hopes for the survival of our system of government. The survival of the government as we know it is the primary assurance to retired persons that Social Security payments will be paid, for at this point in history it is not conceivable that some future group of governmental leaders would risk the wrath of the people by canceling or reducing the payments due under the Social Security system. The record of the past 35 years showing periodic increases in Social Security benefits to keep pace with inflation indicates a firm and continuing commitment to the program.

So long as our political system produces leaders who are responsive to popular demands, and our government and economy are not at the point of collapse, there will be governmental support for delivering on the promises made concerning retirement benefits. If the government and/or economy are by some chance on the point of collapse, it would be of little comfort to have a private insurance plan. In that situation private companies would not likely long survive nor honor commitments any more than would the government.

FALLACY 88

If we could get loafers off welfare, the number of people on the welfare roles could be reduced by half.

If the aged, disabled, and children would go to work this would be possible. But if this is not deemed desirable, then little can be done to reduce the number on welfare. The welfare distribution by category on a national basis is approximately as follows:

	Percent (rounded)
Children whose parents cannot support them	48
Aged over 65 (mostly women)	29
Mothers of children on welfare	12
Blind, disabled, handicapped	10
Fathers of children on welfare	2

Presumably the children are, or should be, in school and not earning a living. Those over 65 are not usually capable of working at a steady job, or cannot readily find work suitable for their capabilities. Mothers of children have an obligation to care for their children, especially if adequate care is not otherwise available or cannot be afforded. The handicapped cannot be expected to support themselves, except in some few cases where suitable employment can be found. This brings us to the 2 percent who are fathers of children on welfare. Of these about two-thirds are not capable of acquiring the job skills or training required to find employment that will pay enough to make them self-sufficient without welfare assistance. This leaves about one-third of these fathers (0.7 percent of the total) who could find productive work, if available, to provide fully for their families.

In terms of these figures, then, getting the loafers off welfare would reduce the number by less than 1 percent. To make a significant dent in the number would require the aged, the handicapped, children, and mothers to seek employment, but this would not make a very useful distinction between loafers and those who deserve public assistance on welfare.

There have been some proposals made that would require all persons applying for welfare, including mothers, to apply also for employment. The recent experience of New York State, which has initiated this kind of program, is instructive. In a survey of welfare job seekers in New York City it was found that of 1,500 who had registered for work, only 15 (1 percent) had found employment. This is to be expected, even if general unemployment rates become lower than they were at the time of this survey. For the most part people receiving welfare tend to be handicapped in several ways that reduce their employability. They tend to have lower than average skills, lower educational achievement, lower levels of physical and mental well-being because of past inadequacies of nutrition and health care, and fewer credentials that would tend to make them acceptable as employees. There is room for reform in our welfare system. But to assume that putting welfare recipients to work will solve the problem is to ignore most of the basic reasons why people are in need of welfare assistance in the first place.

FALLACY 89

Because those who are poor or on welfare in this country are much better off than the poor in other countries, such as Russia or India, there is no reason for them to complain about their condition.

If the poor or disadvantaged would quietly accept their lot, it is true that it would cause less trouble for the consciences of those who are more advantaged. But it ignores the realities of life in this country to argue that there are no reasons for complaint because conditions for the poor here are relatively better than they are in some other country.

This type of argument is irrelevant for at least two reasons. On the one hand, it ignores the fact that the poor do not live in some other country, but live in this one. Because they live here they share most of the images and expectations of American life. These images stress that well-being and an acceptable life style require the ability to purchase a wide variety of goods and services; including two or three cars per family, a big house, many convenience appliances, a college education for the children, vacations to exotic places, and the latest in clothes and hair styling. One would have to live as a hermit to escape the constant bombardment on the senses of these life style images. Radio, television, newspapers, magazines, books, school lessons, and observations of other people, all contribute to the molding of expectations or the setting of standards concerning what it means to live in the United States. When people are constantly exposed to these life style images, but cannot afford even a few modest elements of them, and start to raise questions about the justice of it all, it seems rather beside the point to argue that in absolute terms the people in Russia or India are worse off. The relevant point of reference for the poor is the population of this country, and how their condition compares with the national average for goods and services. If the poor are relatively well off compared to this average, so much the better.

But if they are not very well off, they are well justified in complaining about a situation which leaves them out of the mainstream of American life, when the system itself leads them to expect to be included.

On the other hand, the argument that the poor of other countries are more deprived than those in this country is often used as a tactic to avoid an examination of real problems confronting our own system. Any social or economic system will have some people in a more advantaged situation than others. But if the discrepancies become too great, or if those at the top arrived there by devious or irrational means—as usually happens in any system that survives more than a couple of decades—then there are well-justified grounds for complaint about the system which allows these injustices to continue. In this situation those who benefit from the existing structure of rewards usually point out that things are not really so bad when compared to conditions in other countries; and find this easier, and more self-serving, than undertaking reform of the system to eliminate unnecessary deprivations of the poor.

FALLACY 90

Health care in the United States is the best in the world.

For those who can afford it, the best health care in the world is for sale in the United States. But for those who cannot afford it, a sizable portion of the population, the best health care is not readily available in the United States.

In terms of infant mortality rates, one important measure of health care, the United States ranks fifteenth among the nations of the world. The national average in 1970 was about 22.5 infant deaths per 1,000 live births. This average is an important yardstick for comparing national standards of health care. But within the country there are some striking facts not revealed by the average. The nonwhite infant death rate is now nearly 90 percent greater than for whites—38.8 per 1,000 live births as against 20.6 for whites. One slum neighborhood in Boston has an infant death rate of 111.1 per 1,000 live births while a nearby affluent suburb has only 7.2 infant deaths per 1,000 births. These figures become more understandable in the light of official reports from governmental agencies which show that out of 3.5 million births occurring annually in the United States, at least 500,000 of the women have received inadequate prenatal care, or none at all. In addition to the problem of uneven availability of health care, it should also be noted that the United States, the wealthiest nation in the world, ranks fifteenth in ratio of doctors to population. There is some improvement being made in increasing the number of doctors per capita in the United States. But whether the increase in numbers of physicians improves health care only for the privileged rather than for the disadvantaged is a separate problem requiring more far-reaching changes than simply improving upon the overall doctor-patient ratio.

These data reveal that much needs to be done to provide adequate health care for all Americans, and not just for some Americans. Until this is done the United States, although the wealthiest country in the world, will continue to trail other countries in this important aspect of providing for the general welfare of the people.

FALLACY 91

The only way to help workers hurt by the importation of cheap foreign goods is to raise tariff levies or to impose import quotas or restrictions.

Tariffs and quotas have long been used by this country to protect industries threatened by competition from abroad. These measures are usually self-defeating, however, especially when used by an advanced industrial country such as the United States. Restrictions on imports lead to retaliation by other countries. This means that some other industry is injured by reduced export revenue. Such restrictions also mean that higher prices must be paid for goods purchased by Americans as well as by people in other countries.

There are alternatives available, especially for a country of our technological and productive capacity. This rich potential enables the government to pursue policies other than restricting imports. The most logical alternative, given our resources, facilities, and educational levels, is for government to undertake to retrain people from noncompetitive industries to pursue other occupational tasks and to help them move to a new locality if that is necessary for employment. These things are done in other industrialized countries such as Sweden where unemployment rates are kept below 2 percent, and most of the unemployed are engaged in some kind of training program. We could also encourage failing industries to take advantage of technological innovations and undertake production of products which use our scientific expertise and our pool of highly trained or retrained workers. In this way consumers here and abroad could benefit from lower prices on imported goods and have products made available which were not previously on the market. It would also permit each nation to produce and sell abroad those goods which it is best equipped to manufacture. This would be not only a more efficient use of skills and material resources, but would facilitate that mutual cooperation of nations which has become so necessary in a world facing universal problems of war, pollution, and overpopulation.

FALLACY 92

The more than $100 billion spent on foreign aid since 1946 has produced few benefits in the less developed countries of the world.

Between 1946 and 1965, before the Vietnam war reached its height, the United States expended some $116 billion in overseas loans and grants. Contrary to popular belief, little of this went to help the economic development of less developed countries. About $35 billion was military aid, not economic aid; and was directed at efforts geared to preserve governments favorable to the United States. Approximately $25 billion went to various types of post World War II reconstruction in the more developed countries of Europe and Asia. Some $13 billion was Marshall Plan aid to our West European allies. Therefore, about $43 billion, not $100 billion, was used as economic aid to the less developed countries of the world.

Why has the aid program brought few results in developing countries? The answer is that it has brought results related to types of expenditure and levels of expenditure. Economic recovery aid to Europe in the 1948–1952 Marshall Plan period was very successful, but this assistance spending was at the annual rate of $20 per person. Economic assistance rates in developing countries have been only about $2 per person, so we might well expect less spectacular results. Besides receiving lower rates of aid, the non-European countries have fewer educational and resource advantages to build upon, and primarily have received loans rather than grants of money. Their rates of economic growth, therefore, are bound to be slower. Where military aid is concerned the results have been somewhat better for short-range American interests. Only a few developing countries receiving such aid have assumed an openly anti-American posture. But even where they have not become antagonistic to United States policy it might well be argued that such aid has done little to benefit the people living in those countries.

All in all the American aid program has brought about the basic results intended in terms of the priorities established. These priorities were first, economic recovery of Europe; second, buildup of defense against communist threats around the world; third, assistance (primarily military) to friendly governments to keep them in power; and last, assistance for economic development in the less developed countries of the world.

FALLACY 93

Once military personnel are committed to a military struggle we are morally and patriotically bound to approve of that commitment so long as the president deems it necessary.

"Support our boys in Vietnam." How often has that familiar phrase been heard? Did this mean that opposition to the war effort indicated lack of support for the troops who were suffering and dying in that struggle? Some politicians tried to justify that position, primarily because it is easier to rally support for men in battle than to rally support for the policy which places them in battle.

It is possible, indeed probable, that in this age of confrontation and escalating wars, when policy makers try to use military means to solve political-military problems, as was being done in Vietnam, the best support for the welfare of our troops might well be opposition to policies which place them and our nation in jeopardy in irrelevant struggles. One can oppose military policies and at the same time be concerned for the welfare of troops in battle. Indeed, if there are empirical or moral reasons for objecting to military policies being pursued by the government, it would be one's duty to advocate those objections in an attempt to change policy. To do less would be both unpatriotic in terms of American democracy, and immoral in terms of the lives and safety of the men in battle.

FALLACY 94

If a majority among senators and congressmen disapproves of a presidential commitment of troops in a foreign land, there is no good reason why Congress cannot limit the president by refusing to vote funds for that military venture.

It is true that Congress has the authority to control the purse strings. By reviewing the appropriation requests of the executive it can veto executive policies by refusing to fund them. How does this work as a check on war policy? Not well at all. It does not work because the president and supporters of the war policy would claim that those voting against funds for the war were guilty of not supporting the troops in battle. Even though this would not be true, as noted in the fallacy above, many voters would believe that it is true. Since what voters believe (whether it is accurate or not) affects election outcomes, most congressmen would be unwilling to risk a misunderstanding on the part of the voters by voting against military appropriations. The fact that Congress has authority to veto presidential policy by withholding funds, therefore, does not mean that they will readily use that authority to veto presidential military policy.

FALLACY 95

The best way to achieve a stable world among the major nations is for the United States to maintain military superiority over all potential enemies.

It is comforting to think that one's country has the largest military force in the world, but this ignores some important factors in international relationships.

On the one hand, a policy of military supremacy prompts the leaders of nations fearful of the United States to expand their arms capacity in an attempt to match that of the United States. The Soviet Union has been committed to this at least since 1965. If the United States continues to attempt to keep ahead of its competitors the ensuing arms race will be costly, but will result in no more security for either side, since both sides will be in about the same relative position of strength after a period of arms expansion. The result of such a struggle for supremacy is usually less security from the outbreak of war. An arms race to develop or to maintain superiority tends to produce hostility as well as military armaments, and these hostilities, based upon real or imagined threats, make war more likely as disputes arise and the arms race continues.

On the other hand, a policy of military supremacy tends to prevent other strategies from being pursued that may better lead to a stable and peaceful world. Arms races are costly. As long as one side insists on supremacy there will be little incentive to come to agreement to end the competition of stockpiling armaments. This will mean, in turn, that money and other resources will not be available to use in other ways to promote international and national security. Military power, as the United States is coming to learn the hard way in Vietnam, is not the only or most relevant means to solve all problems in international affairs. Political stability and social justice are closely related, especially in this century. Trying to impose political stability on a country without achieving justice and the allegiance of the people, as we appear to be attempting in Vietnam, is a difficult if not impossible and immoral policy. As William Inge has observed, a man may build himself a throne of bayonets, but he cannot sit on it. If money and resources are available to assist countries to meet their social and economic problems—assistance at a level commensurate with the problems at hand—then alternatives other than military solutions might well be available. If the arms race were ended, the money saved would open the door to these other possibilities. It might also increase awareness of solutions to international problems that do not involve military threats or actions.

Because of these factors, then, a policy of military superiority does not appear to be the best answer to world peace and security. A policy of military parity or sufficiency coupled with arms control efforts would likely achieve better results. In this regard it is instructive to note that in the 1970s, when the United States rejected the idea of military superiority, a lowering of hostility emerged. With that altered policy and other world developments the United States and the Soviet Union were able to come to agreement on arms limitations and a moderation of, if not an end to, the arms race.

FALLACY 96

By reading a key book or article one can gain a firm understanding of a political or social problem and the knowledge of solutions to that problem.

Political and social problems are usually very complex because they involve many people with differing value commitments and varying empirical circumstances. To understand a particular problem, therefore, usually requires a rather extensive background of information which is seldom provided by any one book or journal article.

To find solutions to problems requires an application of value positions or choices to the empirical situation. Any one book or article will necessarily be selective in both factual information presented and value commitments expressed or implied. To arrive at a useful solution to a political or social problem, therefore, will require exposure to a variety of sources of information, at least as a first step. This will enable the reader to place the issue in a context that will facilitate a better understanding of implications, and increase the ability to rationally judge proposed solutions.

As an aid to rational judgment in general, it is usually better to judge information, whether obtained by reading or by other means, in the wider context of different information sources and of one's own previous knowledge and value preferences. At times this may lead to the acceptance of a new value position as well as an altered policy stance. At other times one's original position may be reinforced. In any case it seems wise to be wary of accepting any one information source as the fount of all wisdom.

This skepticism or caution obviously applies to this book as well as to any other source of information. It is hoped, however, that most (if not all) of the conclusions reached herein will survive the test of the reader's judgment.

SELECTED REFERENCES FOR FURTHER STUDY

Baldwin, David A. *Foreign Aid and American Foreign Policy: Documentary Analysis.* New York: Praeger Publishers, 1966.

Baldwin reviews the first twenty years of the American foreign aid program since World War II. The study includes reports from a variety of congressional and presidential commissions on foreign aid policy, and other commentaries on successes and failures.

Editorial Research Reports on the Urban Environment. Washington, D.C.: *Congressional Quarterly,* 1969.

A collection of reports covering major problems facing the cities. Among those reports are studies of population growth, urban violence, welfare reform, and local government modernization.

Greenberg, Selig. *The Quality of Mercy: A Report on the Critical Condition of Hospital and Medical Care in America.* New York: Atheneum, 1971.

Greenberg details many of the gaps between promise and practice in the delivery of health care in the United States. The discrepancies include those between the health care available to whites and that available to blacks, the gap between national per capita income which is highest in the world and the national infant mortality ranking which is fifteenth, the disparity between the relatively high proportion of GNP spent on health care and the higher male life expectancy of 21 other countries.

Harrington, Michael. *The Other America: Poverty in the United States.* New York: Macmillan Co., 1962.

In the affluent society of the United States there are 40–50 million poor people who are without adequate food, housing, education, or health care. The poor are invisible to most Americans because of the many ways to mask poverty. Special problems of the aged and the black population are examined. Because the welfare state was designed to ease the suffering of the middle class and does not reach the poor, a major effort will be needed to improve conditions for the latter. The effort must be comprehensive so that both the material conditions of poverty and the culture of poverty are attacked and the vicious circle of circumstance is broken.

Lefever, Ernest W., ed. *Arms and Arms Control.* New York: Praeger Publishers, 1962.

This collection of essays examines the conditions and tactics of arms control. The discussion is premised on the emerging consensus of opinion that concerns the stability of the present nuclear stalemate based upon our second strike capability to deter attack. In these circumstances arms control becomes a viable goal. Tactics include projection of a less militant attitude, self-restraint to induce reciprocal action, and traditional negotiations. Common interests in limiting the arms race make collaboration between adversaries possible. It is generally agreed that stability and prevention of war cannot be imposed by military dominance, but that it is a reciprocal endeavor best pursued by arms control collaboration in the face of rising costs of an arms race.

Lockard, Duane. *The Perverted Priorities of American Politics.* New York: Macmillan Co., 1971.

In concluding sections of the book, Lockard offers some suggestions as to why our national priorities seem to be perverted and what should or can be done to correct them. He notes that if badly conceived policies can gain public support, then perhaps better ones can also gain support if they are demonstrated to further long-run self-interest.

Morgenthau, Hans J. *Politics Among Nations: The Struggle for Power and Peace.* 5th ed. New York: Alfred A. Knopf, 1972.

In addition to a general survey of international politics and the general principles involved in the interaction of nations in both peace and war, this book includes some interesting comments on the problems and prospects of balance of power and arms control policies.

Ulmer, Melvin J. "How Unfair Are Our Taxes." *New Republic,* 7 November 1970, pp. 17–19.

Ulmer attempts to document the fact that taxes levied on the wealthy are not as high as would be supposed after looking at the top income tax rates. He suggests that the tax system does not progressively tax high income as it should.

The following journal articles are part of the ongoing analysis of some of the topics examined in this chapter.

Coffey, J. I. "Strategic Superiority, Deterrence, and Arms Control." *Orbis,* 13 (Winter 1970):991–1007.

Daly, George, and Giertz, Fred. "Welfare Economics and Welfare Reform." *American Economic Review,* 62 (March 1972):131–38.

Daniels, Robert. "Future of Medical Care Delivery Systems." *Social Service Review* 45 (Sept. 1971):259–73.

Dougherty, James E. "Arms Control in the 1970's." *Orbis* 15 (Spring 1971): 194–217.

Mott, Basil J. F. ed. "Crisis in Health Care: Problems of Policy and Administration." *Public Administration Review* 31 (Sept. 1971):501–42.

Rushing, William A. "Public Policy, Community Constraints, and the Distribution of Medical Resources." *Social Problems,* 19 (Summer 1971):21–36.